FRETBOARD ROADMAPS ALTERNATE GUITAR TUNINGS

THE ESSENTIAL GUITAR PATTERNS THAT ALL THE PROS KNOW AND USE

BY FRED SOKOLOW

THE RECORDING
Guitar and Other Stringed Instruments and Vocals—Fred Sokolow
Sound Engineer, Bass and Other Instruments—Michael Monagan
Recorded at Sossity Sound

with editorial assistance by Ronny Schiff

ISBN 978-1-4234-7995-6

7777 W. BLUEMOUND RD. P.O. BOX 13819 MILWAUKEE, WI 53213

In Australia Contact:
Hal Leonard Australia Pty. Ltd.
4 Lentara Court
Cheltenham, Victoria, 3192 Australia
Email: ausadmin@halleonard.com.au

Visit Hal Leonard Online at
www.halleonard.com

CONTENTS

INTRODUCTION

The standard guitar tuning is (low to high) E–A–D–G–B–E, but guitarists of many genres have retuned the guitar in a number of ways for various reasons. Alternate tunings were used by the early acoustic blues players like Blind Willie McTell and Robert Johnson, and early country-folksters like Maybelle Carter and Doc Watson. Early rockers Bo Diddley and Don Everly (of the Everly Brothers) and folk-rockers Joni Mitchell and Bob Dylan widened the scope of alternate tunings. Sixties guitar heroes Jimi Hendrix, Eric Clapton, and Jimmy Page, and rockers of subsequent decades like Nirvana, U2, Soundgarden, Metallica, System of a Down, and singer/songwriters like Elliott Smith and Nick Drake all adapted alternate tunings to their styles. Today's metal, hard rock, and indie artists often retune. (See **ROADMAP #13** for more info on which players use the various tunings.)

To play in alternate tunings, you have to learn new chord shapes and scales. So, why bother? Here are just a few of the reasons to retune:

- Some arrangements are easier to play in an altered tuning.
- The droning sound you get from open tunings suits the mood of many songs.
- Lowered bass strings often make it easier to fingerpick appropriate bass notes.
- Lowered strings give you a darker, heavier sound.
- Lowered strings are easier to bend.
- An unusual tuning makes you think outside the box while composing or arranging a song.

In the pages that follow, you'll learn how to play backup and pick single-note solos in several popular tunings. For each tuning, there are moveable patterns that make it easy.

If you're interested in playing guitar in altered tunings, this book will shed much light and save you a great deal of time. Read on, and many mysteries will be explained.

Good luck,

Fred Sokolow

P.S. Slide guitarists often tune to an open chord. This is covered in another roadmaps book, *Fretboard Roadmaps for Slide Guitar* (Fred Sokolow, published by Hal Leonard Corporation). Also, for more general music theory, see Fred Sokolow's *Fretboard Roadmaps*, published by Hal Leonard.

THE RECORDING AND THE PRACTICE TRACKS

All the licks, riffs, and tunes in this book are played on the accompanying recording. It's very helpful to listen to each tune or exercise before attempting to play it.

Many of the tracks are solo guitar, while some include a backup band. Tracks that include a band are mixed with the guitar on the left side of your stereo and the backup band on the other side. This way, you can isolate the guitar for closer study or remove it completely and play along with the backup band.

HOW TO READ CHORD GRIDS

A *chord grid* is a picture of several frets of the guitar's fretboard. The dots show you where to fret (finger) the strings:

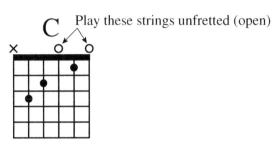

Numbers under a grid indicate the fingering. The number to the right of the grid is a *fret number.*

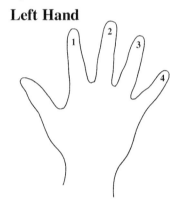

HOW TO READ FRETBOARD DIAGRAMS

Each *fretboard diagram* is a schematic picture of the guitar's fretboard as it appears when you look down at it while playing.
- The sixth, heaviest string is at the bottom; the first, lightest string is on top.
- Crucial fret numbers such as 5, 7, and 9 are indicated underneath the grid.
- Like chord grids, *dots* on the fretboard indicate where you fret the strings.
- *Numbers* on the fretboard indicate which finger to use (1 = index finger; 2 = middle finger; etc.).
- *Letters* on the fretboard are notes (A, B♭, C♯, etc.).
- *Roman numerals* (I, IV, etc.) on the fretboard are roots of chords.

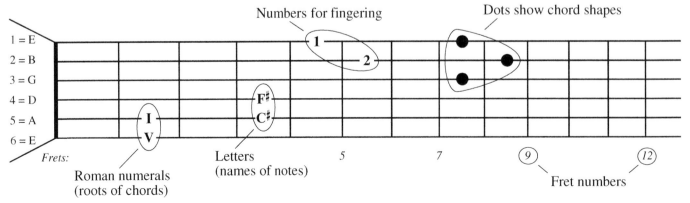

4

HOW TO READ TABLATURE

Songs, scales, and exercises in this book are written in standard music notation and tablature. The six lines of the tablature staff represent the six guitar strings.

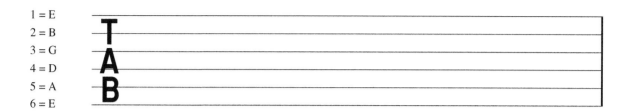

A number on a line tells you which string to play and where to fret it.

This example means "play the third string on the fourth fret"

This example means "play the fourth string unfretted"

Chords can also be written in tablature:

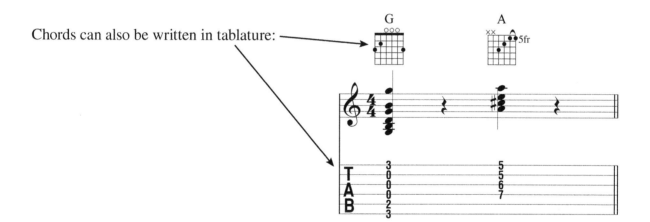

GUITAR NOTATION LEGEND
All the details of tablature notation (hammer-ons, slides, etc.) are explained in the *Guitar Notation Legend* at the back of this book.

NOTES ON THE FRETBOARD

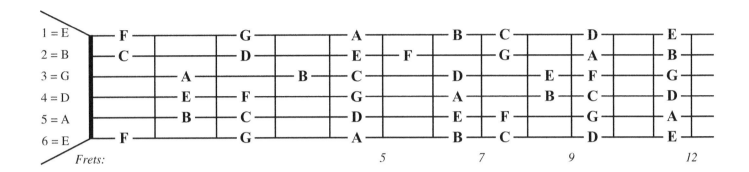

WHY? Knowing where the notes are in standard tuning will help you find chords and scales up and down the neck. It will also give you a frame of reference when you use alternate tunings.

WHAT? **The notes get higher in pitch as you go up the alphabet and up the fretboard.**

A whole step is two frets, and a half step is one fret. Most notes are a whole step apart (e.g., D is two frets above C; E is two frets above D), but there are half steps in two places: B to C is one fret and E to F is one fret.

Sharps are one fret higher: sixth string/third fret = G, so sixth string/fourth fret = G♯; sixth string/eighth fret = C, so sixth string/ninth fret = C♯.

Flats are one fret lower: sixth string/fifth fret = A, so sixth string/fourth fret = A♭; sixth string/tenth fret = D, so sixth string/ninth fret = D♭.

Some notes have two names: sixth string/fourth fret is both G♯ and A♭. The name you use depends on the musical context.

HOW? **Help from fretboard markings.** Most guitars have fretboard inlays or marks somewhere on the neck that indicate the fifth, seventh, ninth, and 12th frets. Be aware of these signposts. Once you've memorized the fact that the sixth string/fifth fret is A, the fretboard mark on fret 5 helps you get there fast.

Everything starts over at the 12th fret. The 12th fret is like a second nut. Three frets above the nut on the sixth string is G; three frets above the 12th fret on the sixth string is G too.

The note names on the sixth and first strings are the same. When you memorize the sixth-string notes, you also have the first-string notes.

DO IT!   **Start by memorizing the notes on the sixth and fifth strings.**

Walk up the sixth string, naming the notes as you go. Start with the letter-only names (F, G, etc.), and then add the sharps and/or flats later.

Spot-check yourself on the sixth string. Play random notes, out of order, naming them as you play them.

Learn the fifth-string notes the same way. Name the notes as you walk up the string, and then spot-check yourself by playing random notes.

Play sixth-and-fourth-string octaves to learn the fourth-string notes.
When you use the hand position shown in the adjacent chord grid to play the sixth and fourth strings simultaneously, the fourth-string note is the same note as the one on the sixth string, only it's an *octave* (eight notes) higher. Once you have memorized the notes on the sixth string, this is a shortcut to learning the fourth-string notes.

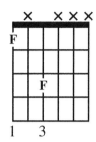

After playing a lot of octaves, walk up the fourth string, naming the notes as you go. Continue using the sixth string as a reference point, and then spot-check yourself on the fourth string the same way you did on the sixth string.

Play fifth-and-third-string octaves to learn the third-string notes. You can relate the third string to the fifth-string notes:

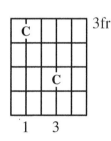

Walk up the second string, naming notes as you go. Then play random notes on the second string, naming them as you play them.

SUMMING UP—NOW YOU KNOW...

1. The location of the notes on the fretboard, especially on the fifth and sixth strings.

2. The meaning of these musical terms:
    a) Sharp (♯)
    b) Flat (♭)
    c) Whole Step
    d) Half Step

DROP D TUNING

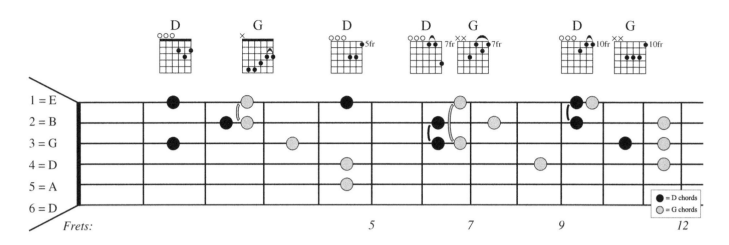

More Chords

WHY? Used by artists as musically diverse as Pete Seeger and Kurt Cobain, *Drop D tuning* offers a low D bass note, enriching the sound when you play a D chord. More importantly, it allows you to play many up-the-neck licks and partial chords in D, still having bass notes to support them.

WHAT? Drop D is the same as standard tuning, except the sixth string is lowered from E to D (D–A–D–G–B–E).

TRACK 1

The above diagram shows many moveable chords that are useful in this tuning.

To get to Drop D tuning from standard tuning, lower the sixth string to D.

HOW? An appropriate open or fretted bass string is indicated for each of the chord shapes in **ROADMAP #2**.

You can also play normal, standard-tuning chords if you omit (don't play) the sixth string:

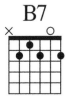 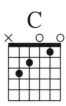  

DO IT! Review and play the chord shapes of **ROADMAP #2.**

Listen to the following tracks while reading the tablature, and then play along with each one.

This arrangement of the classic blues tune "Stagolee" is inspired by the alternating-thumb picking style of the great bluesman Mississippi John Hurt. It illustrates how to play first-position chords in Drop D.

STAGOLEE

TRACK 2

Drop D

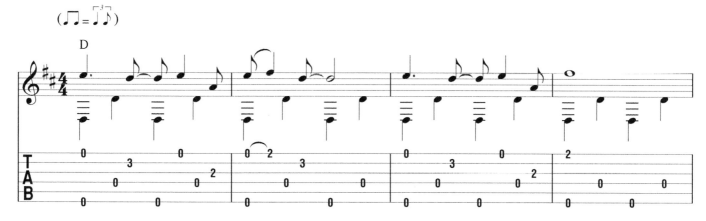

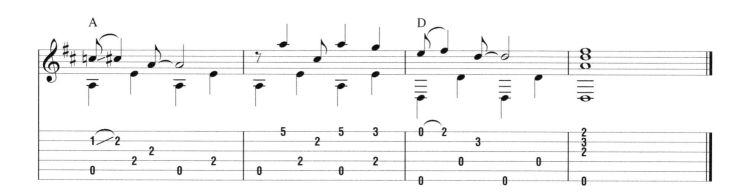

Electric country guitarists sometimes use Drop D in order to play growling, low-register riffs like these:

COUNTRY TWANG

TRACK 3

Here's a rock version of the same low-register concept:

ROCK BASS RIFF

TRACK 4

Rock bands often play grungy, chord-based riffs in Drop D:

HEAVY ROCK CHORD RIFF

TRACK 5

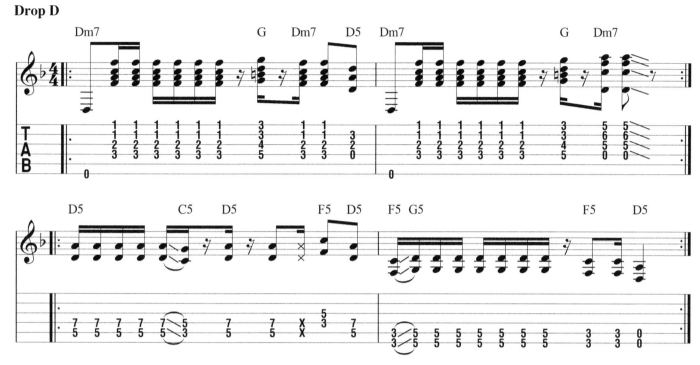

Back now in "acoustic bluesland," this tune shows how to make use of up-the-neck chords in Drop D.

LONESOME BLUES

TRACK 6

"Acoustic Journey" uses many of the same shapes as "Lonesome Blues" in a folk-rock context.

ACOUSTIC JOURNEY

Drop D

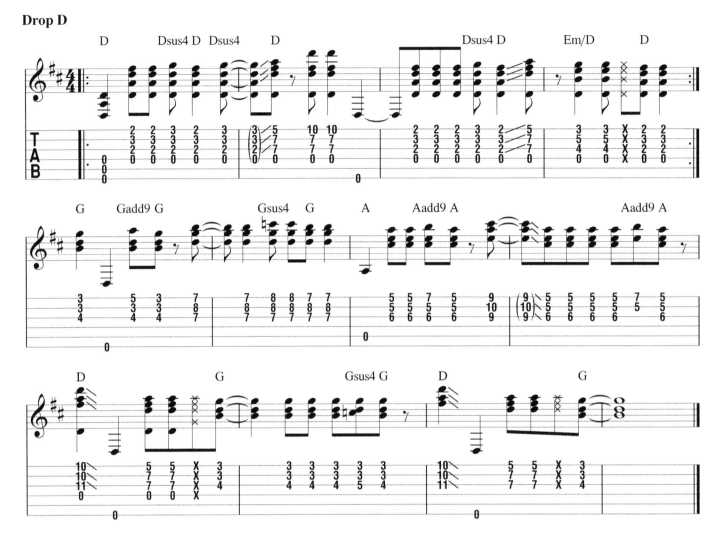

There's also a Drop C tuning, which is standard tuning with the sixth string lowered to C (C–A–D–G–B–E). It offers a low, growling C bass note when you play in the key of C. Here are some useful chord shapes in Drop C:

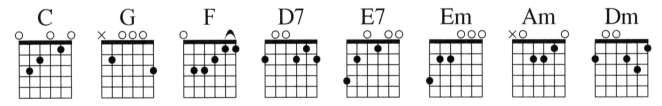

SUMMING UP—NOW YOU KNOW...

1. How to tune to Drop D.

2. How to play many up-the-neck chords in Drop D.

3. Which bass notes to play with each chord shape.

4. How to tune to Drop C and play some chords for that tuning.

OPEN D TUNING: FIRST POSITION

D Major Scale

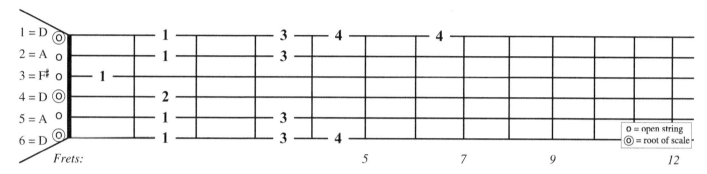

o = open string
(o) = root of scale

More Chords

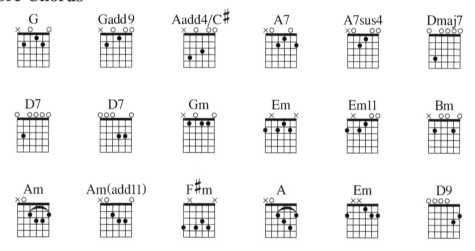

G   Gadd9   Aadd4/C#   A7   A7sus4   Dmaj7

D7   D7   Gm   Em   Em11   Bm

Am   Am(add11)   F#m   A   Em   D9

D Minor Pentatonic Scale

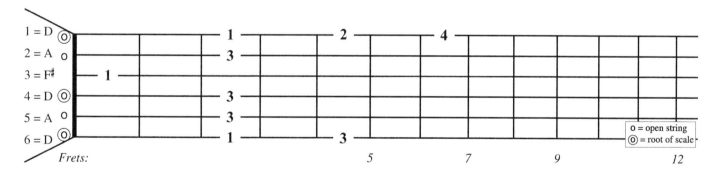

o = open string
(o) = root of scale

WHY? *Open D tuning* is one of the most popular open tunings used by blues, rock, country, folk, and folk-rock artists.

WHAT? This tuning is called Open D because a strum across the open (unfretted) strings results in a D major chord.

To get to Open D tuning from standard tuning:

— Tune both E strings (the first and sixth) down to D.

— Tune the third string (G) down to F♯.

— Tune the second string (B) down to A.

TRACK 8

ROADMAP #3 shows a first-position major scale and some first-position chords in Open D tuning.

The second fretboard diagram shows a first-position D minor pentatonic scale. The *minor pentatonic scale* consists of these intervals: 1–♭3–4–5–♭7.

HOW?

Play the major scale ascending and descending, starting on the sixth string.

Do the same with the minor pentatonic scale.

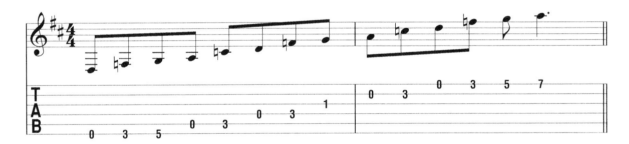

Practice playing the chord shapes.

DO IT!

Use this tuning's scales and chords to play the following songs. "The Water Is Wide" is an old folk tune that uses many first-position chords.

THE WATER IS WIDE

TRACK 9

Open D tuning

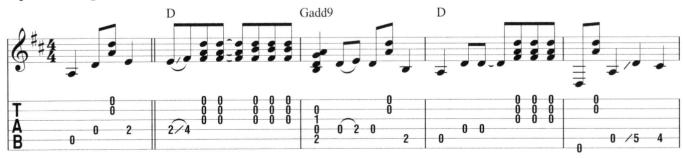

"Amazing Grace" is played in two registers. The A at the seventh fret is an example of the simple, two-finger chord fragments often used in this tuning. The two-note chord sounds full when supported by the open A (fifth) string.

AMAGING GRACE

TRACK 10

Open D tuning

This fingerpicking version of the folk tune, "Nine Pound Hammer," features an alternating-thumb bass line while the fingers play the melody on the treble strings. Notice the up-the-neck lick—it shows how you can continue playing bass notes while picking a melody in the higher registers.

NINE POUND HAMMER

TRACK 11

Open D tuning

"Stone Blind" shows how you can use the Open D tuning to create bluesy, gnarly rock riffs.

STONE BLIND

Open D tuning

TRACK 12

This version of the old folk-blues tune, "Chilly Winds," is inspired by the playing of acoustic blues masters like Skip James and Blind Willie McTell. A lot of blue notes and seventh chords create a bluesy, lonesome atmosphere.

CHILLY WINDS

Open D tuning

TRACK 13

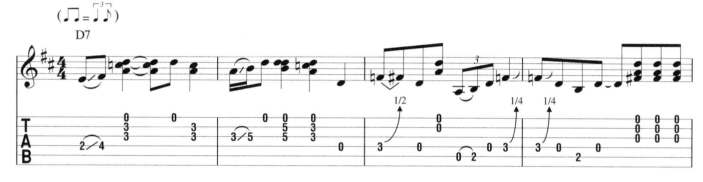

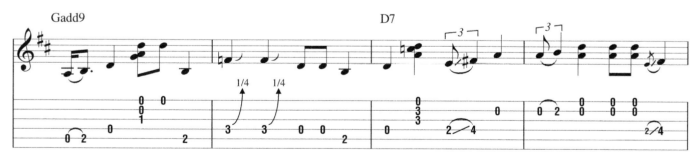

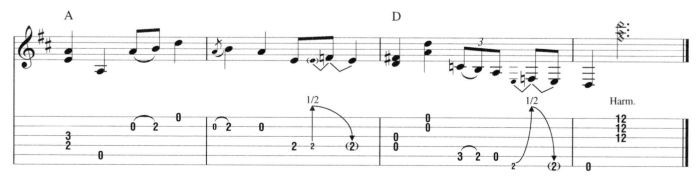

SUMMING UP—NOW YOU KNOW...

1. How to tune to Open D.

2. How to play first-position D major and D minor pentatonic scales in Open D tuning.

3. How to play several first-position chords and a few up-the-neck chord fragments in Open D tuning.

4. How to play backup in Open D tuning for several musical genres (rock, blues, country, and folk).

5. How to play first-position melodic solos in Open D tuning.

OPEN D TUNING: MOVEABLE CHORDS

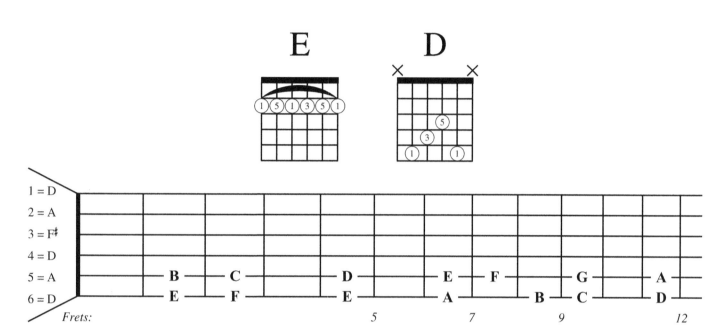

WHY?   You can base solos and backup on moveable chords and play all over the fretboard in Open D tuning.

WHAT?   **ROADMAP #4 shows two moveable chords in Open D tuning.** The E chord has a sixth-string root, and the D chord has a fifth-string root. (The *root* is the note that gives the chord its name. An E note is the root of an E chord.)

The numbers in the large chord grids are *intervals*. Every major chord is composed of a root, 3rd, and 5th of the chord's major scale. A C chord is composed of the notes C–E–G, as these are the first, third, and fifth notes of the C major scale.

The large grids illustrate which notes in the two moveable major chords are roots, 3rds, and 5ths.

The fretboard chart shows the notes on the sixth and fifth strings. Learning these will help you play moveable chords all over the fretboard.

HOW?   Practice playing the moveable chord positions, naming them as you play, and then practice switching from one chord to another.

Start with the major barre chords, as they are the easiest to play.

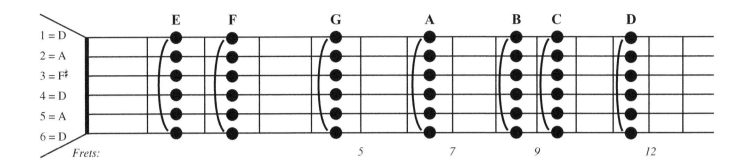

Play the fifth-string-root, moveable major chords in several places on the fretboard, naming them as you go.

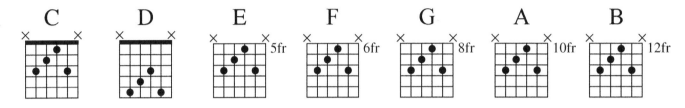

Locate the minor, seventh, and other chord types by relating them to the major barre chords. By changing one or two notes of a barre chord, you can create many other moveable, sixth-string-root chords:

Sixth-string root

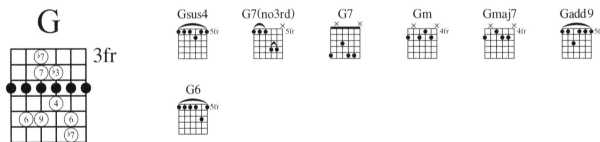

Locate more minor, seventh, and other chord types by relating them to the moveable, fifth-string-root chord:

Fifth-string root

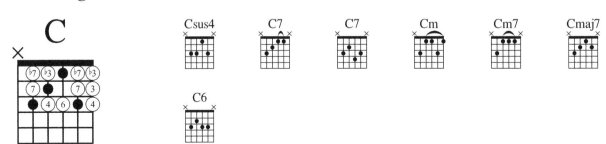

DO IT!   **Play the following rock variation of "Chilly Winds." It uses a number of moveable chords.**

CHILLY WINDS #2

TRACK 14

Open D tuning

Play chord-based backup to "The Water Is Wide #2," which has many chord changes, major and minor.

Strum Pattern:

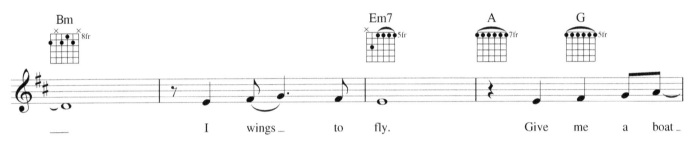

THE WATER IS WIDE #2

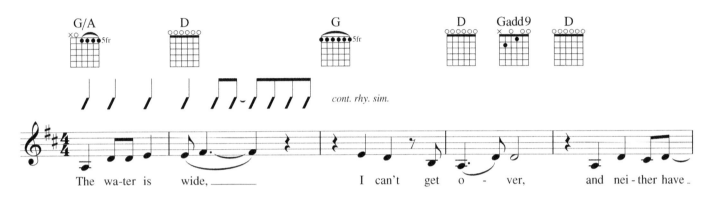

The wa-ter is   wide, _____   I   can't   get   o - ver,   and   nei - ther have ___

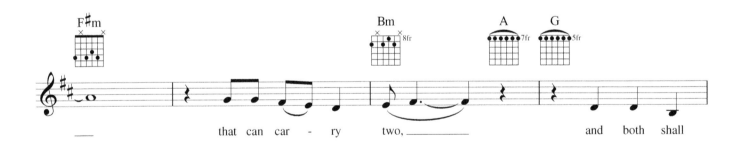

___   I   wings ___   to   fly.   Give   me   a   boat ___

that   can   car - ry   two, _____   and   both   shall

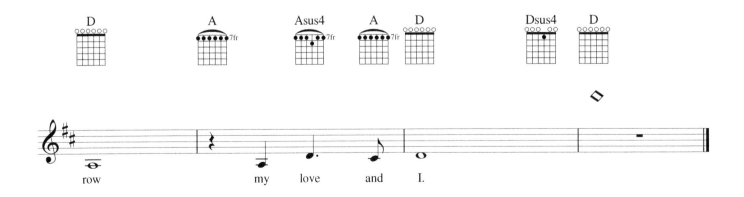

row   my   love   and   I.

This rock ballad riff is based on barre chords and their variations: *sus4* (root–4th–5th) and *add9* (root–3rd–5th–9th) chords. It's reminiscent of the Rolling Stones and other classic blues-rock bands.

BLUE SUSPENDERS

TRACK 16

Open D tuning

SUMMING UP—NOW YOU KNOW...

1. How to play all the major barre chords in Open D tuning.

2. How to make the major barre chords into minor, seventh, and other chord types.

3. How to create chord-based rock riffs in Open D tuning.

OPEN D TUNING: I–IV–V CHORD FAMILIES

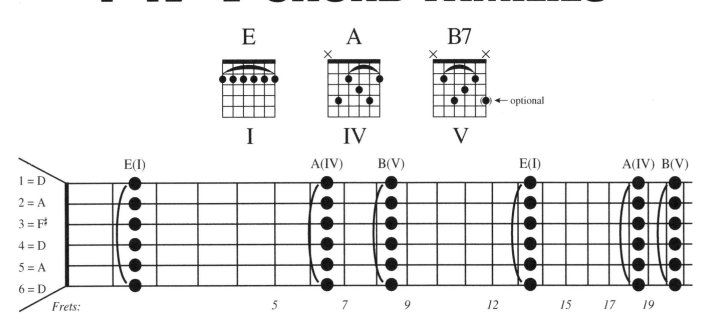

WHY? Thousands of songs have three-chord progressions. Those three chords are usually I, IV, and V. That's why it's useful to know two ways to play the I–IV–V chord progression in any key in Open D tuning.

WHAT? **Musicians often use Roman numerals to describe chord progressions.** These refer to intervals of the major scale. D is the first note of the D major scale, and E is the second note. So, in the key of D, D is the I chord, and Em is the ii chord.

The I, IV, and V chords (e.g., D, G, and A in the key of D) are closely related and are often called a "chord family."

ROADMAP #5 shows a I–IV–V barre chord family in the key of E. The E chord is I, the A is IV, and the B is V.

The IV chord is always five frets above the I chord, as shown in the fretboard diagram of ROADMAP #5.

The V chord is always two frets above the IV chord.

Everything starts over at the 12th fret. The open strings are tuned to a D chord in Open D tuning, so a barre at the 12th fret is also a D chord. A barre at the second fret is E, so a barre at the 14th fret (two frets above the 12th fret) is also an E. That's why two I–IV–V barre chord families in E are shown in **ROADMAP #5**: one at the second fret and the other at the 14th fret.

The chord grids show another way to play a I–IV–V chord family. In this method, all three chords (I, IV, and V) are played within the same three frets.

HOW? To find the IV chord of any barre chord, play the same shape five frets higher. For example, a barre at the fifth fret is a G chord. A barre at the 10th fret is the IV chord (C) in the key of G.

To find the V chord of any barre chord, play the shape seven frets higher (or two frets above the IV chord). Since a barre at the fifth fret is G, a 12th fret barre (D) is the V chord.

Here's another way to play I, IV, and V chords:

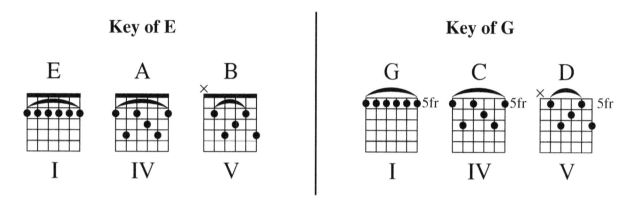

The IV chords above resemble a suspension of the I chord and are sometimes used as such. *Sus4 chords* use the 4th interval instead of the 3rd (i.e., E is E–G♯–B, Esus4 is E–A–B).

For example, Esus4 resembles an incomplete A chord:

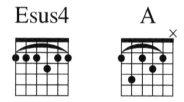

Because they are similar, IV is often substituted for Isus4, as the following riffs illustrate:

SUSPENSION RIFFS

TRACK 17

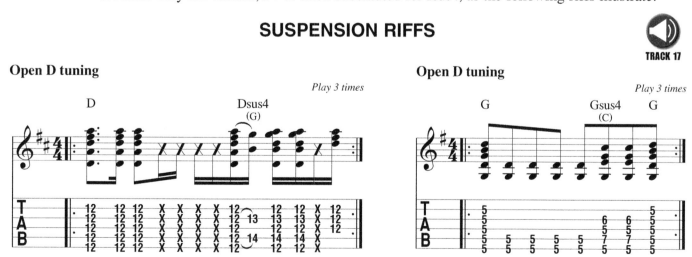

It's easy to play a bluesy, boogie-bass lick in Open D tuning, working off the major barre chords. This lick is played on the lower two strings:

BOOGIE BASS LICK

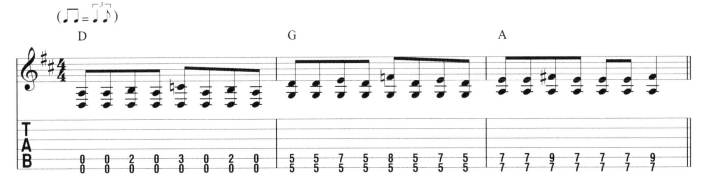

DO IT! "Boogie Shuffle in D" makes use of I, IV, and V barre chords in the key of D. It's not unlike the backup part Elmore James's rhythm guitarist (his cousin, Homesick James) often used in blues tunes. Note the classic blues turnaround (last two measures) at the end of the 12-bar progression. Many 8- or 12-bar blues progressions end with a *turnaround*: a brief musical phrase, usually ending on the V chord, that sets up a repeat of the progression.

BOOGIE SHUFFLE IN D

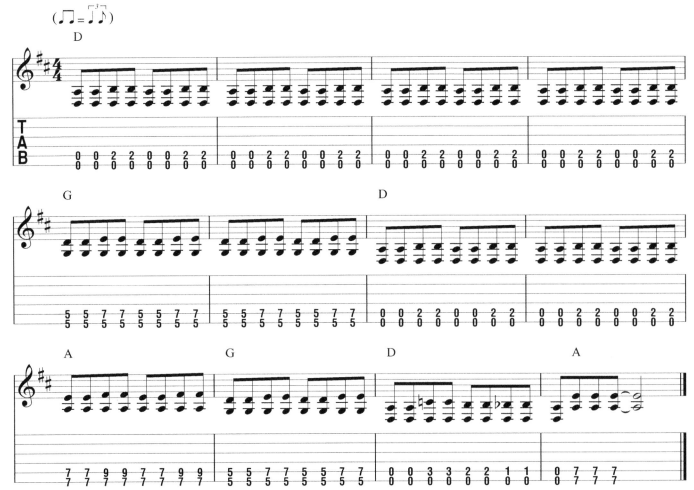

"Detox" makes use of the sixth-string-root barre chord in the key of G. (You don't have to play in the key of D just because you're in Open D tuning!) Some sus4 and add9 chords and bass/boogie licks are used in this classic rock progression. *Add9* chords contain the intervals root–3rd–5th–9th (the 9th is the same note as the 2nd). For example, Gadd9 contains the notes G–B–D–A.

DETOX

TRACK 20

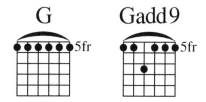

Open D tuning

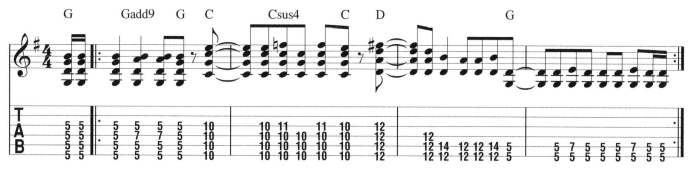

Here's the same tune using the chord grid shapes from **ROADMAP #5:**

DETOX #2

TRACK 21

Open D tuning

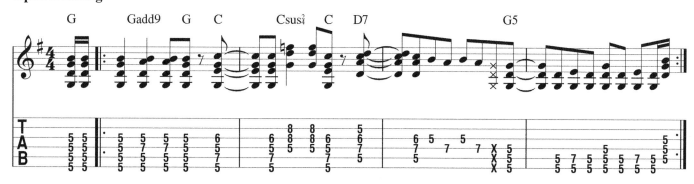

Move that IV chord up two frets, and you have another way to play the V chord:

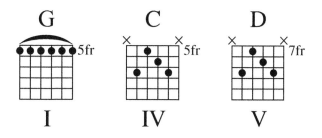

The following fingerpicked ballad shows how to use this type of V chord.

INNER SPACES

Open D tuning

SUMMING UP—NOW YOU KNOW...

1. What I–IV–V chord families are.

2. Two ways to find and play IV and V chords in relation to the barre I chord.

3. How to play bass/boogie licks in Open D tuning.

4. A third way to locate the V chord.

OPEN G TUNING: FIRST POSITION

G Major Scale

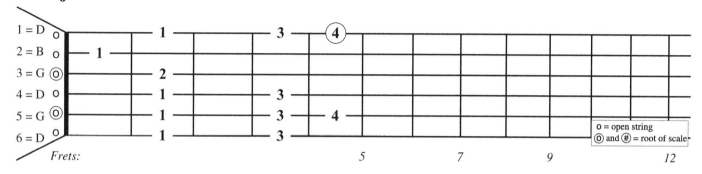

More Chords

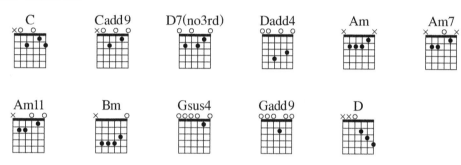

G Minor Pentatonic Scale

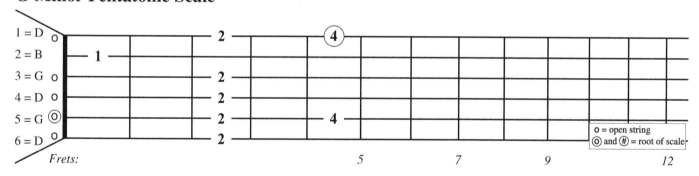

WHY? Some of the first blues guitarists ever recorded played in *Open G tuning*, and the tuning has been picked up by country artists, rockers, and folk-rockers. It's as widely used as Open D.

WHAT? This tuning is called Open G because a strum across the open (unfretted) strings results in a G major chord.

To get to Open G tuning from standard tuning:

— Tune both E strings (the first and sixth) down to D.

— Tune the A (fifth) string down to G.

TRACK 23

ROADMAP #6 shows first-position G major and G minor pentatonic scales and some first-position chords in Open G tuning.

HOW? Play the major scale ascending and descending, starting on the sixth string.

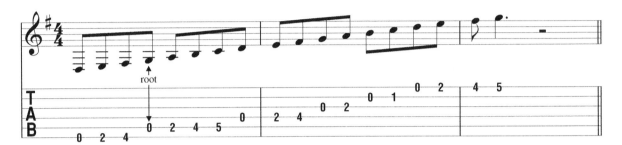

Do the same with the minor pentatonic scale.

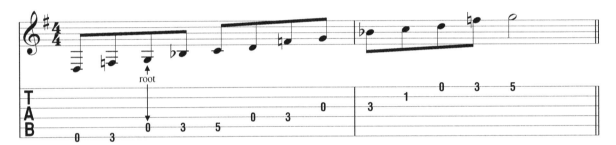

Practice playing the chord shapes.

DO IT! Use the G major scale and first-position chords to play "No Hiding Place." This is an old gospel tune arranged in the style of early blues fingerpickers like Furry Lewis, Mance Lipscomb, and Mississippi John Hurt. The fingers pick a major scale-based melody on the treble strings while the thumb plays an alternating bass.

NO HIDING PLACE

TRACK 24

Open G tuning

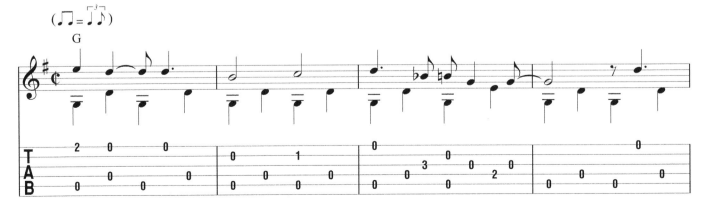

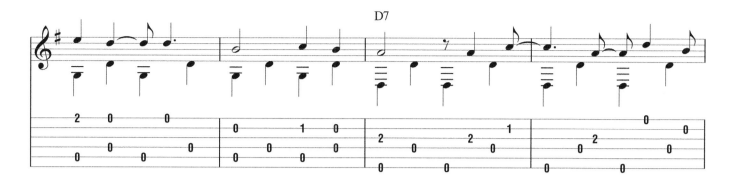

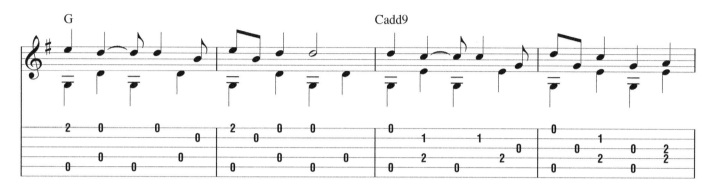

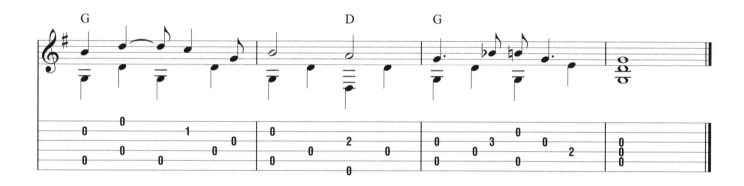

The following instrumental makes use of the **G minor pentatonic scale.** It's in the style of Robert Johnson and other fingerpicking blues players of the 1930s, and it features a sporadic, monotone bass backup.

IN THE EVENING

**Open G tuning**

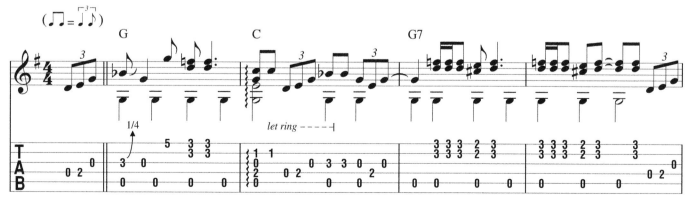

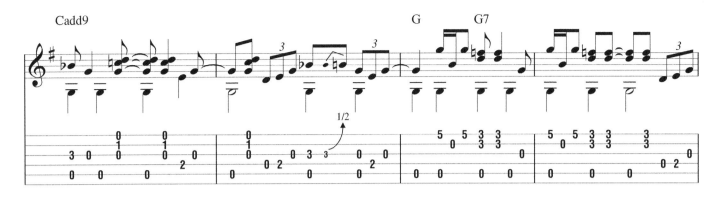

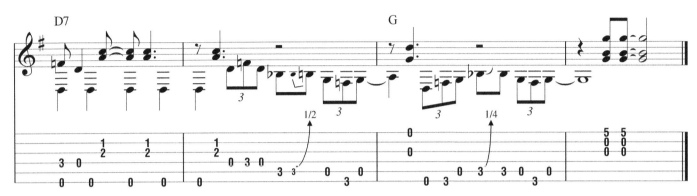

Blues licks from "In the Evening" can be used to create a hard rock groove. Just add some distortion and a straight-eighths feel, as the following solo illustrates:

ROCKING IN THE EVENING

TRACK 26

Open G tuning

This version of "The Water Is Wide" has a gentle folk-rock feel. The melody is based on the major scale. The open strings in many of the first-position chords create suspensions, minor ninths, and other interesting harmonies.

THE WATER IS WIDE #3

TRACK 27

Open G tuning

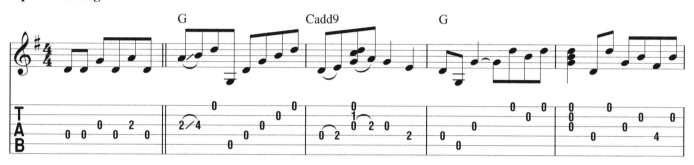

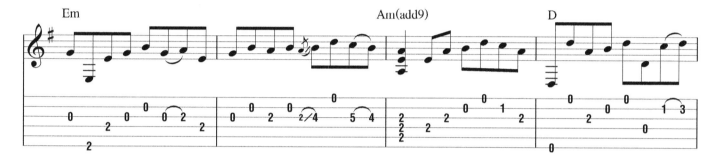

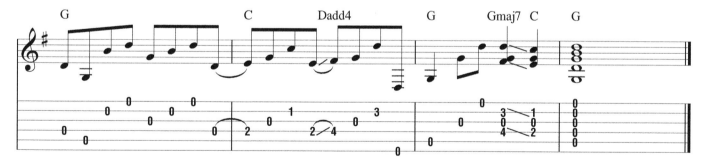

SUMMING UP—NOW YOU KNOW...

1. How to tune to Open G.
2. How to play first-position G major and G minor pentatonic scales in Open G tuning.
3. How to play several first-position chords in Open G tuning.
4. How to play melodic solos and backup in first-position Open G tuning for several musical genres (blues, rock, and folk).

OPEN G TUNING: MOVEABLE CHORDS

G

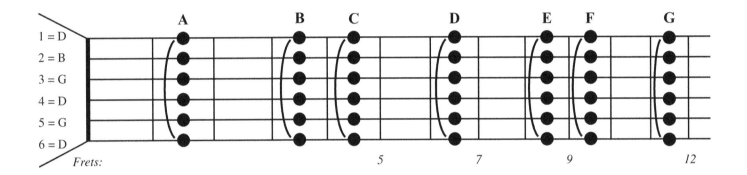

WHY? In Open G tuning, just as Open D tuning, you can base solos and backup on moveable barre chords.

WHAT? **ROADMAP #7 shows barre chords in Open G tuning.** Notice that the fifth string is the root of the chord in this tuning (unlike Open D where the sixth string is the root). Once you memorize the barre chords up and down the fretboard, you've learned the notes on the fifth string.

The chord grid shows the intervals of a barre chord, so you can alter the shape to create other chord types. The numbers represent intervals.

HOW? Practice playing the barre chords all over the fretboard, naming them as you go.

Locate minors, sevenths, and other chord types by relating them to the major chord, as you did in Open D tuning (**ROADMAP #4**):

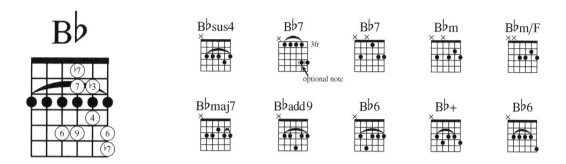

DO IT! This fingerpicking blues piece makes use of moveable major, seventh, and sixth chords (*sixth chords* are triads with an added 6th interval). It's in the style of Mississippi John Hurt and John Fahey, both of whom often used Open G tuning.

DONE GONE

TRACK 28

Open G tuning

Ever since "Honky Tonk Women," Keith Richards has played in Open G tuning, creating classic riffs like those in "Brown Sugar" and "Start Me Up." The following version of "Nine Pound Hammer" demonstrates some typical Keith moves, including sus4 and add9 chords, as well as boogie bass.

NINE POUND HAMMER #2

Open G tuning

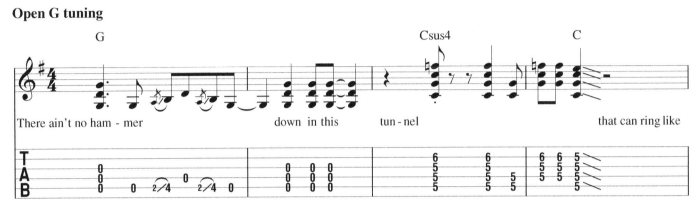

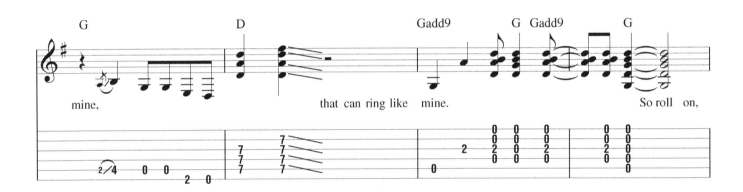

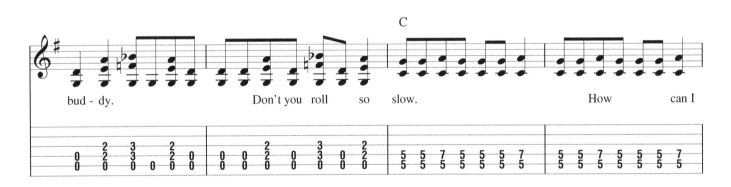

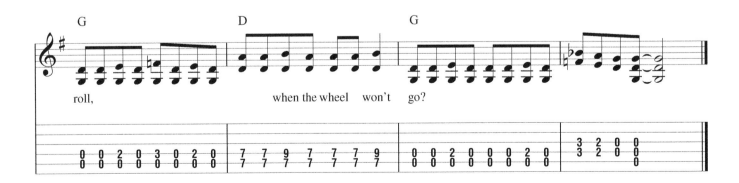

This instrumental, based on an old Tin Pan Alley tune, makes use of several moveable chords, including sixth, minor, and add9 voicings. The arrangement is somewhat reminiscent of Hawaiian slack key guitar, which will be discussed in the next chapter.

PRETTY BABY

TRACK 30

Open G tuning

SUMMING UP—NOW YOU KNOW...

1. How to play all major barre chords in Open G tuning.

2. How to make major barre chords into minor, seventh, and other chord types.

3. How to play solos and backup, up and down the fretboard, based on moveable chords in Open G tuning.

OPEN G TUNING: I–IV–V CHORD FAMILIES

G Chord Families

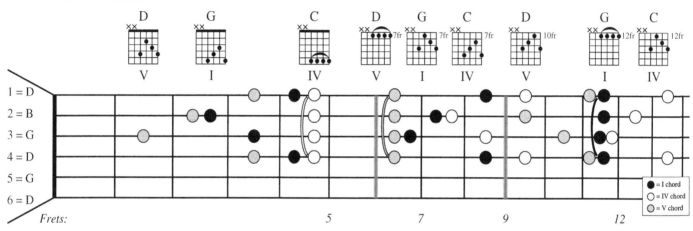

WHY? Knowing how to play chord families automatically all over the fretboard makes it easy to navigate the neck in Open G tuning.

WHAT? There are three moveable chord formations in the above diagram: F, D, and Barre shapes.

F formation   D formation   Barre

ROADMAP #8 shows how to arrange these chord shapes into three I–IV–V chord families in the key of G.

Once you've memorized these chord families, you can automatically make I–IV and I–V moves in several different registers, in the same key.

HOW? **These chord relationships are moveable!** They are useful in any key. For example, in the key of D, you can play these three D chord families:

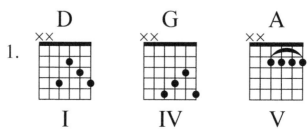

1.   D   G   A
      I   IV   V

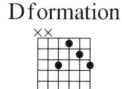

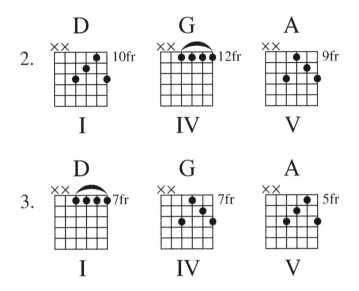

In any key, the three I chords (the D, Barre, and F chord formations) have the same ascending pattern on the fretboard. It's a loop that goes:

— From the D formation, skip two frets to...

— Barre formation. Skip two frets to...

— F formation. Skip one fret to...

— D formation, and so on, until you run out of frets.

All the D Chords

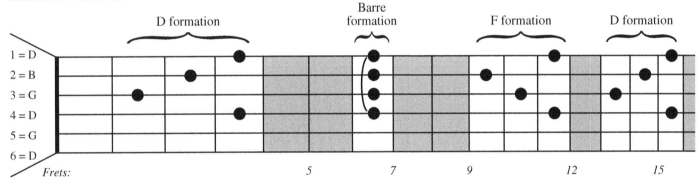

You can use the **D–Barre–F ROADMAP** to follow any chord up the neck and play all the G, A, C, or D chords automatically.

All the A Chords

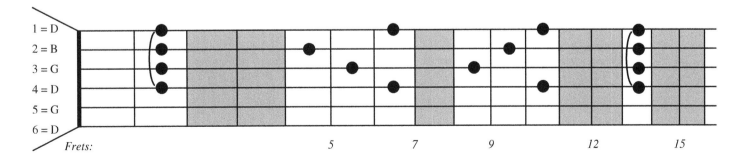

Once you fully assimilate ROADMAP #8 and combine it with the D–Barre–F ROADMAP, you can play three different I–IV–V chord families in three different registers, in any key.

DO IT! **Hawaiian slack key guitar players often use Open G. They call it "taro patch tuning."**
Slack key is another way of saying "some strings are tuned to a lower pitch," but it has come to
denote Hawaiian acoustic fingerstyle. "Taro Patch" is in the slack key style. Notice the use of
the open D and G strings with the partial chords, all derived from **ROADMAP #8**.

TARO PATCH

TRACK 31

Open G tuning

The following arrangement of the old folk tune, "Goin' Down That Road Feelin' Bad," shows
how to make use of **ROADMAP #8** in a fingerpicking country-blues.

GOIN' DOWN THAT ROAD FEELIN' BAD

TRACK 32

Open G tuning

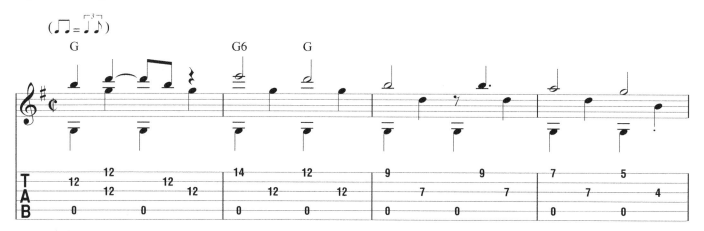

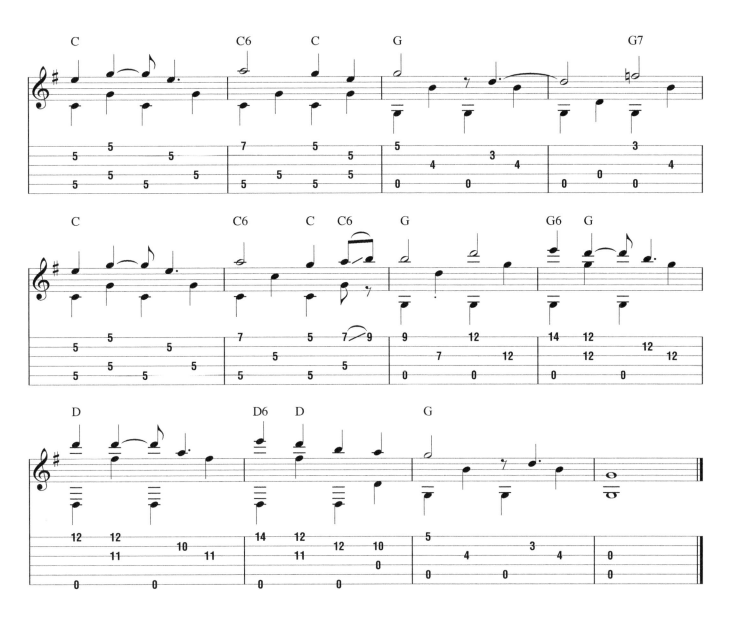

In the reggae progression below, the rhythmic chop chords draw upon the various roadmaps of this chapter. (*Chop chords* are percussive strums that are muted right after they sound.)

REGGAE PROGRESSION

TRACK 33

Open G tuning

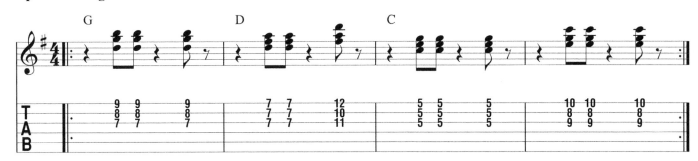

SUMMING UP—NOW YOU KNOW...

1. How to play three I–IV–V chord families all over the fretboard in any key.

2. How to play one chord all over the fretboard, in high and low registers, using three moveable, major-chord formations.

OPEN G–A AND D–E TUNING CONVERSIONS

Open G Tuning - Minor Pentatonic Scale

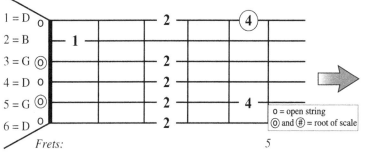

Open A Tuning - Minor Pentatonic Scale

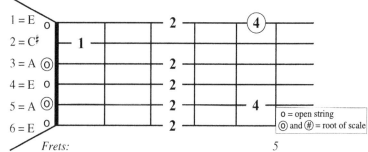

Open D Tuning - Minor Pentatonic Scale

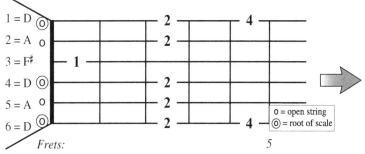

Open E Tuning - Minor Pentatonic Scale

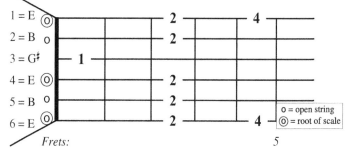

WHY? Open A and Open E are popular tunings among blues, slide, country, rock, and folk guitarists. You can quickly navigate these tunings if you understand their relationship to Open G and D tunings, respectively.

WHAT? *Open A tuning* **is the same as Open G, but every string is tuned a whole step (two frets) higher.** Robert Johnson sometimes used this tuning, both with and without a slide.

In Open A tuning, you can play all the Open G tuning licks, scales, chords, and solos. The names of the chords and scales change, but the chord shapes and fretboard roadmaps are the same.

Open E tuning is the same as Open D, but every string is tuned a whole step higher.

In Open E tuning, you can play all the Open D licks, scales, chords, and solos. As in the Open G–A tuning relationship, names change, but fingering patterns are identical.

HOW?

To get to Open A tuning from Open G, tune every note up two frets.

TRACK 34

To get to Open A tuning from standard tuning:

— Tune the fourth string up two frets, to E. Match it to the open sixth string.

— Tune the third string up two frets, to A. Match it to the open fifth string.

— Tune the second up two frets, to C♯. Match it to the newly-tuned third string, fourth fret.

To get to Open E tuning from Open D, tune every note up two frets.

TRACK 35

To get to Open E tuning from standard tuning:

— Tune the fifth string up two frets, to B. Match it to the open second string

— Tune the fourth string up two frets, to E. Match it to the open sixth string.

— Tune the third string up one fret, to G♯. Match it to the newly-tuned fourth string at the fourth fret.

When you play Open G solos or licks in Open A, they are in the key of A, and the names of chords and notes move up two frets. The G minor pentatonic scale fingering is now an A minor pentatonic scale; barre at the fifth fret is D instead of C, and so on.

The same goes for playing Open D solos or licks in Open E. The names of notes and chords move up two frets.

DO IT!

Play a solo in Open E using Open D tuning scales and chords. For example, here's an Open E version of "Blue Suspenders," from **ROADMAP #4**:

BLUE SUSPENDERS IN E

TRACK 36

Open E tuning

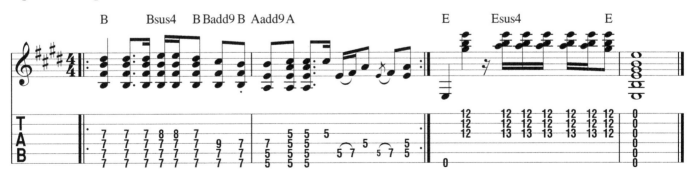

Play a solo in Open A using Open G tuning scales and chords. Here's "Done Gone," from **ROADMAP #7**, played in Open A:

DONE GONE IN A

TRACK 37

Open A tuning

SUMMING UP—NOW YOU KNOW...

1. How to tune to Open A and E.

2. How to play in Open A by relating it to Open G tuning.

3. How to play in Open E by relating it to Open D tuning.

OPEN G–D TUNING CONVERSION

Open G Tuning - IV Chord

Open D Tuning - IV Chord

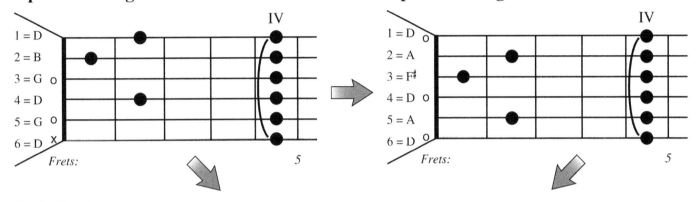

Both Tunings

WHY? There's a relationship between Open G and D tunings that makes it possible for you to borrow licks or solos from one and use them in the other.

WHAT? **In both tunings, barre chords have the same interval relationships on the fretboard.** In both tunings, the I chord is open and at the 12th fret, the IV chord is at the fifth fret, the V chord is at the seventh fret, and so on (II chord at the second fret, III chord at the fourth fret; see *Fretboard Roadmaps* for more on these relationships).

In Open D, you can use Open G tuning licks, scales, solos, and chords if you move them down a string. An Open G lick that is played on strings 1 and 2 can be played in Open D on strings 2 and 3. That's because the string-to-string intervals on the top five strings (first–fifth) of Open G match those on the bottom five strings (second–sixth) of Open D tuning.

Similarly, you can steal many Open D ideas and use them in Open G tuning by moving them *up* a string. Any Open D lick or chord that doesn't use the first string is eligible for this conversion.

Moving the IV Chord Up a String

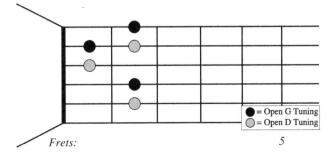

45

HOW?   When in Open D tuning, play an Open G lick by pretending the second string is the **first string of that tuning with the actual first string missing.** Here are some Open G turnarounds converted to Open D tuning. Note that the chords, as well as the licks, are moved up a string.

TRACK 38

Open G tuning

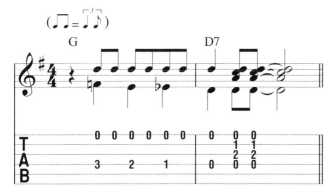

Open D tuning

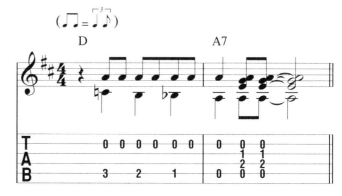

Open G tuning

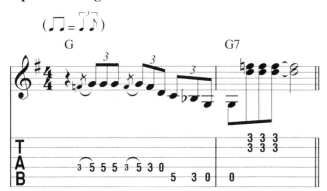

Open D tuning

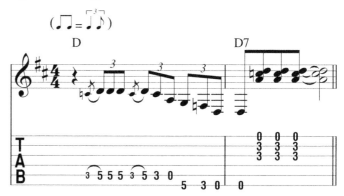

When in Open G tuning, play an Open D lick by moving it down a string. An Open D lick on the sixth and fifth strings translates over to Open G tuning on the fifth and fourth strings, as this boogie lick on the bass strings illustrates:

TRACK 39

Open D tuning

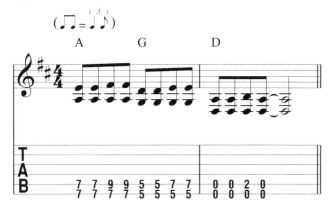

Open G tuning

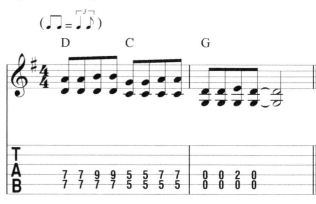

DO IT! Here's "No Hiding Place" in Open D tuning, transposed from the Open G version from **ROADMAP #6.** It's almost the exact same solo as in that chapter, just moved up a string.

NO HIDING PLACE IN D

TRACK 40

Open D tuning

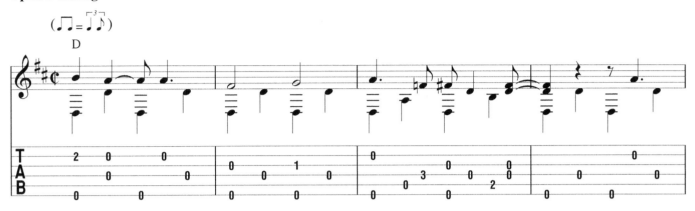

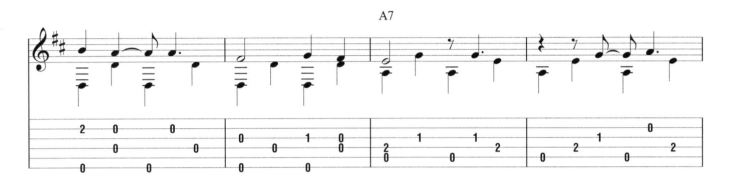

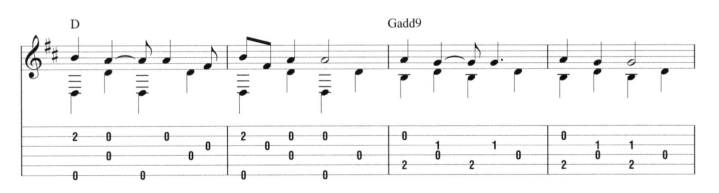

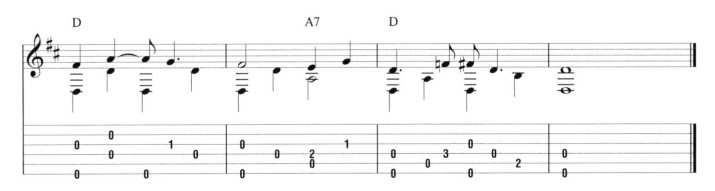

Here's "The Water Is Wide" in Open G tuning, adapted from the Open D version from the **ROADMAP #3** chapter.

THE WATER IS WIDE IN G

TRACK 41

Open G tuning

SUMMING UP—NOW YOU KNOW...

1. How to convert Open G licks, solos, and chords to Open D tuning.

2. How to convert Open D licks, solos, and chords to Open G tuning.

DADGAD: FIRST POSITION

D Major Scale

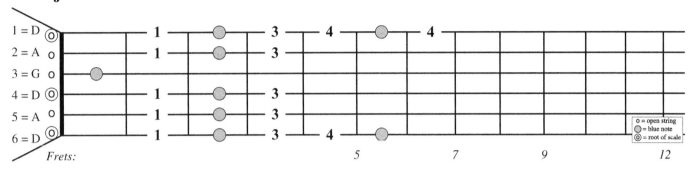

More Chords

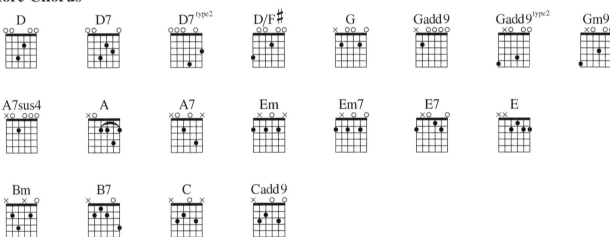

WHY? *DADGAD* tuning (sometimes called "D Modal") is often associated with Celtic music, as it was first popularized by British and Irish guitarists who often use it to play jigs, reels, and traditional Irish tunes. DADGAD has also been used in rock, folk, blues, and pop music, proving to be very versatile.

WHAT? **ROADMAP #11** shows the DADGAD tuning, a first-position D major scale (the numbers), and some first-position chords.

The gray dots are blue notes (♭3rds, ♭5ths, and ♭7ths).

DADGAD is exactly like Open D tuning, except the third string is tuned up one fret higher to G. This creates a Dsus4 chord when all the open strings are strummed.

To get to DADGAD from standard tuning:

— Tune both the E strings (first and sixth) down to D (you can match them to the fourth string).

— Tune the B string (second) down to A (you can match it with the fifth string).

TRACK 42

HOW?

Practice the D major scale:

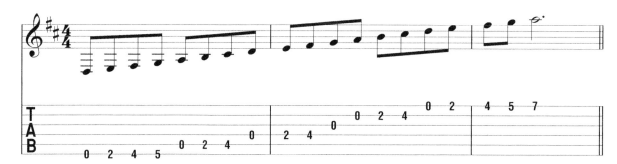

Practice the first-position chords and switch from one to the other.

DO IT!

Play the traditional Irish jig "The Irish Washerwoman." It's a good workout in D major, and the occasional open D and A strings make the single-note melody line complete. Like most jigs and fiddle tunes, this one has two sections, each played twice in a row.

THE IRISH WASHERWOMAN

TRACK 43

DADGAD

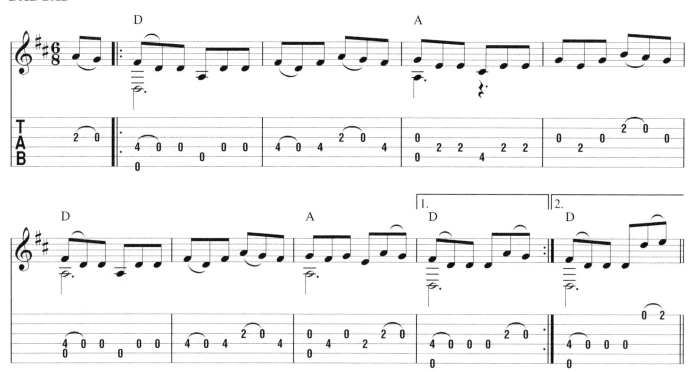

Melodies can often be played up the neck (in higher registers) in DADGAD with minimal chording. Here's a high-register arrangement of the first section of "The Irish Washerwoman." It makes use of only one up-the-neck chord shape—and it only uses three fingers!

THE IRISH WASHERWOMAN #2

TRACK 44

DADGAD

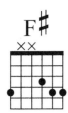

"Aura Lee" uses most of the first-position chords from ROADMAP #11. It's an old Irish folk tune that inspired Elvis Presley's "Love Me Tender." This arrangement makes use of one moveable chord, F♯.

AURA LEE

TRACK 45

DADGAD

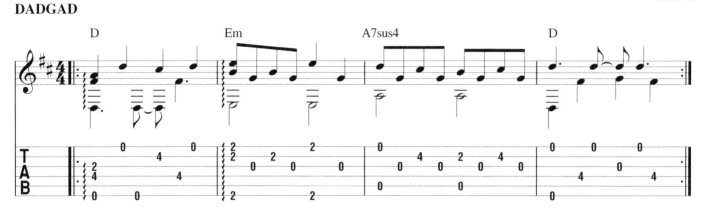

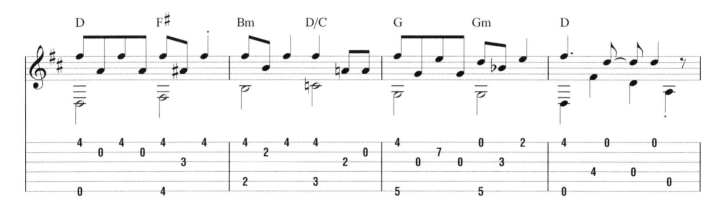

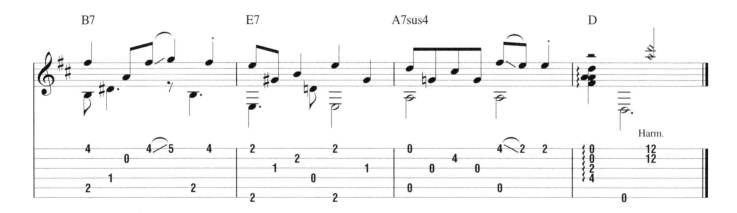

The following arrangement of "Londonderry Air," sometimes known as "Danny Boy," makes use of many first-position chords and features the droning quality that is often associated with DADGAD. The use of many open strings causes this drone effect.

LONDONDERRY AIR

TRACK 46

DADGAD

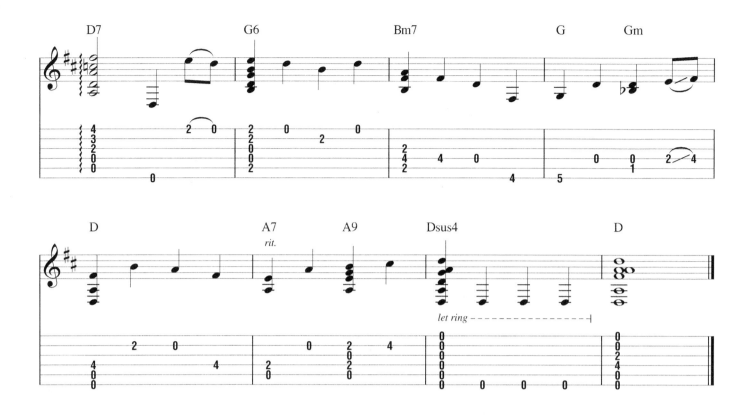

DADGAD is also suited to blues playing. Practice the D minor pentatonic scale below, and then play the instrumental version of "Two White Horses." It's in the same vein as the old blues, "See That My Grave Is Kept Clean," also known as "One Kind Favor."

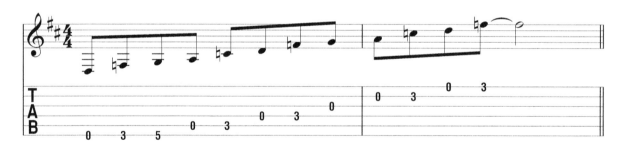

TWO WHITE HORSES

DADGAD

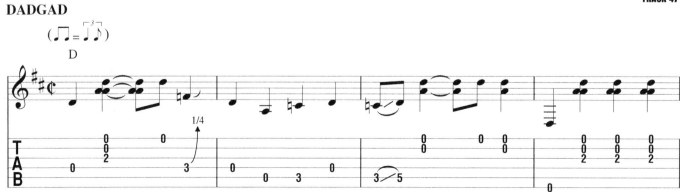

SUMMING UP—NOW YOU KNOW...

1. How to tune to DADGAD.

2. How to play first-position D major and D minor pentatonic scales in DADGAD.

3. How to play first-position melodies and chords in DADGAD.

DADGAD: MOVEABLE CHORDS

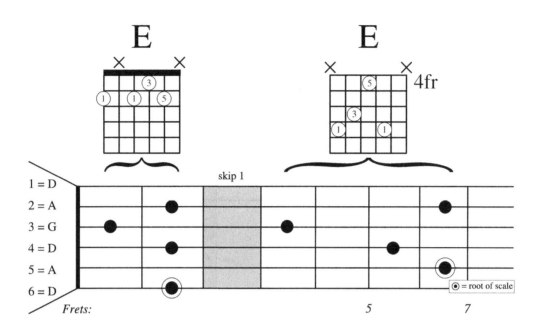

WHY? Although DADGAD is associated with chords that include open strings, as in **ROADMAP #11**, many players use moveable chords to play in any key all over the fretboard. The moveable chords in **ROADMAP #12** make DADGAD a versatile tuning.

WHAT? **ROADMAP #12** shows two moveable E chords, one with a fifth-string root and one with a sixth-string root.

The numbers in the chord grids are *intervals* (**1, 3, or 5**).

DADGAD differs from Open D tuning by only one note (the third string is tuned to G instead of F♯), so many DADGAD chords will closely resemble those learned in **ROADMAP #4**.

HOW? If you know the notes on the fifth (A) and sixth (D) strings, as shown in **ROADMAP #4**, you can play the moveable chords from **ROADMAP #12** all over the fretboard. For example:

F Major Chord Shape

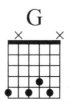

D Major Chord Shape

D
2fr

F
5fr

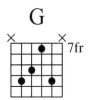
G
7fr

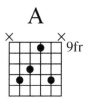
A
9fr

You can alter the two moveable chords of ROADMAP #12 to create many different chord types. Here are some chords that are derived from the sixth-string-root moveable major chord:

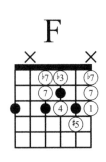
F

F

Fmaj7

Fmaj7^{type2}

Fm

Fm^{type2}

Fm7

Fm7^{type2}

F7

F7^{type2}

Fsus4

F+

Here's how to alter the fifth-string-root moveable major chord to create different chord types:

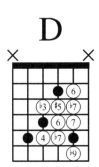
D

D6

D6^{type2}

D7

D7
4fr

D7^{II}

D7♭9
4fr

D9
4fr

D9^{II}

Dm7

Dm6

D7$\sharp$5

D+

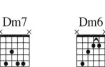

Since so many songs are composed of I–IV–V chords, it's helpful to be familiar with the moveable I–IV–V chord relationships in DADGAD (or any tuning). In any key, if you start on a I chord with a sixth-string root, the I–IV–V chord family looks like this:

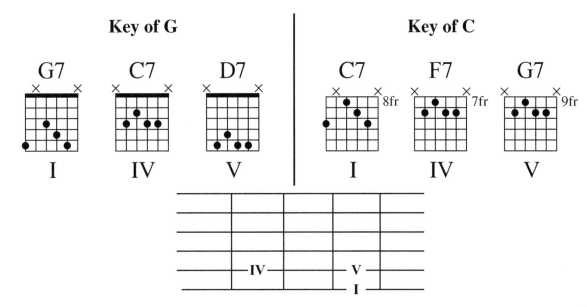

Key of G

G7   C7   D7
I   IV   V

Key of C

C7   F7   G7
8fr   7fr   9fr
I   IV   V

IV   V
I

If you start on a I chord with a fifth-string root, the I–IV–V chord family looks like this:

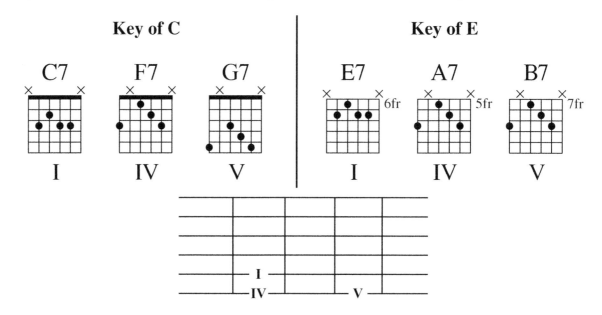

DO IT! To practice the I–IV–V relationships, strum this eight-bar blues in G. In the first eight measures, the I chord has a sixth-string root, and in the second eight measures the I chord has a fifth-string root.

DADGAD BLUES

TRACK 48

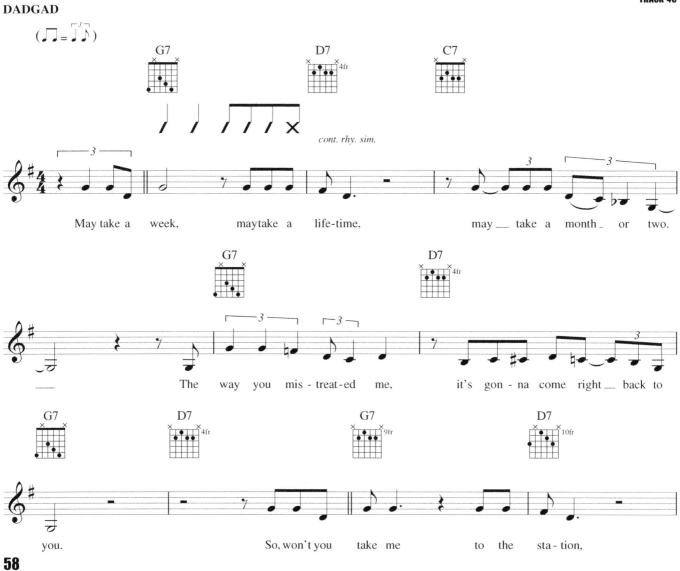

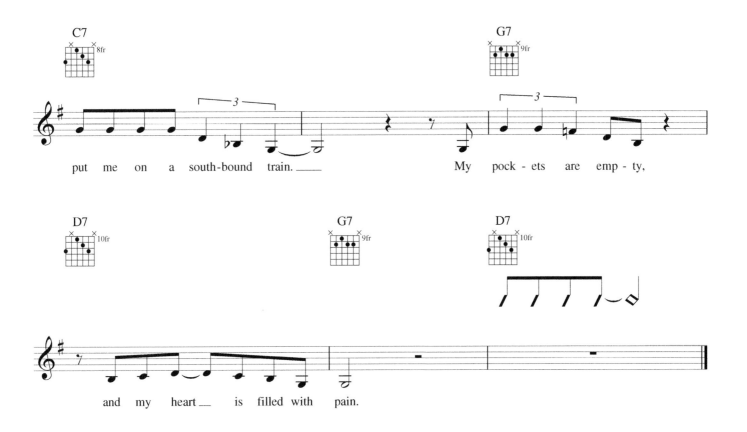

put me on a south-bound train. _____   My pock - ets are emp - ty,

and my heart _____ is filled with pain.

Here's another popular chord progression played with moveable chords. It's often referred to as "the rhythm changes," because it resembles Gershwin's "I Got Rhythm," but it's the basis of countless jazz tunes from the 1920s through contemporary popular music. The first eight measures are similar to "Heart and Soul," "Oh Donna" (and countless other doo wop ballads), "Stand By Me," "Be My Baby," "Everybody's Got a Hungry Heart," and "Every Breath You Take."

DADGAD RHYTHM

TRACK 49

DADGAD

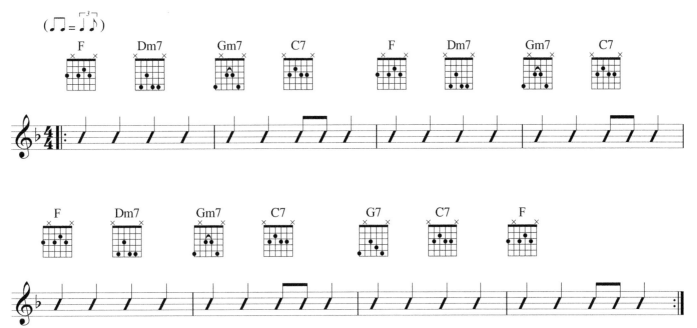

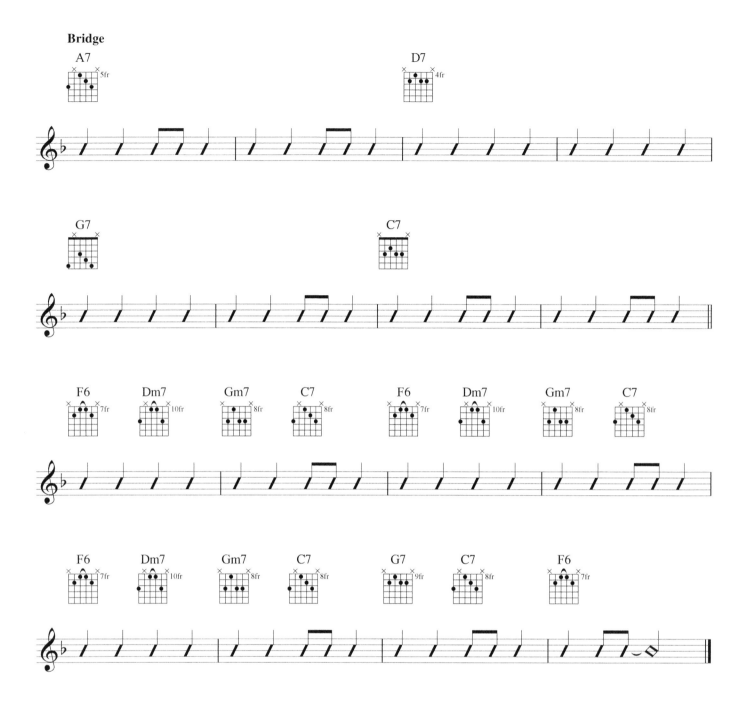

Here's a very old pop tune played with moveable **DADGAD chords.** It's arranged in *chord melody style* (the chords and melody are played simultaneously).

LET THE REST OF THE WORLD GO BY

TRACK 50

DADGAD

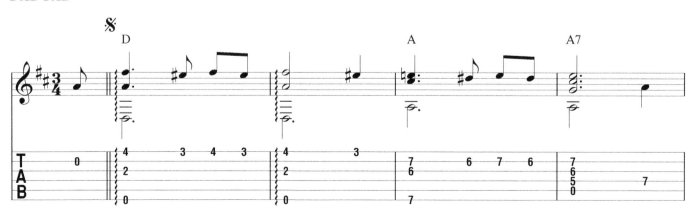

SUMMING UP—NOW YOU KNOW...

1. How to play two moveable major chords in DADGAD all over the fretboard.

2. How to alter those major chord shapes to create many different chord types (sevenths, minors, etc.).

3. How to play I–IV–V progressions in any key, two different ways in each key, using moveable chords in DADGAD.

4. How to play the "the rhythm changes" using moveable chords in DADGAD.

5. How to play in chord melody style using moveable DADGAD chords.

WHO USES WHICH TUNING?

Here are some examples of how contemporary guitarists and legendary players of decades past have made use of altered tunings:

Standard tuning, two frets lower (D–G–C–F–A–D): Used by Alice in Chains, the Beatles ("Yesterday"), Black Sabbath, Elliott Smith, Guns N' Roses, Metallica, Nirvana ("Come as You Are"), Pantera ("Walk"), and Soundgarden.

Standard tuning, four frets lower (C–F–B♭–E♭–G–C): This is *the* heavy metal tuning. Tony Iommi used it (but tuned a fret higher) on most of Black Sabbath's *Masters of Reality* album. Other players include Billy Corgan (Smashing Pumpkins), Soundgarden ("Fourth of July"), System of a Down, John Mayer ("Neon"), and the Who ("Underture"). Queens of the Stone Age almost always use it. Maybelle Carter tuned this way on "Can the Circle Be Unbroken" and often tuned three or four frets down, as do many twelve-string guitarists, including Jimi Hendrix on "Hear My Train A Comin'."

Drop D (D–A–D–G–B–E): Some famous users of this tuning include Radiohead ("Optimistic"), Led Zeppelin ("Moby Dick"), Creed ("Higher"), Soundgarden ("Spoonman"), the Beatles ("Dear Prudence"), Jefferson Airplane ("Embryonic Journey"), and Bob Dylan ("It's Alright, Ma [I'm Only Bleeding]").

Drop D tuning, one fret lower (D♭–A♭–D♭–G♭–B♭–E♭): Billy Corgan of Smashing Pumpkins called this "the grunge tuning" and had a special guitar made for it. Others who use it include Linkin Park (most of their songs), Metallica ("Dirty Window"), Nirvana ("Heart-Shaped Box" and "Something in the Way"), and System of a Down.

Drop C (C–A–D–G–B–E): Dylan used it on "It's All Over Now, Baby Blue."

Open D (D–A–D–F♯–A–D): It has been used by Joni Mitchell ("Chelsea Morning"), Bruce Cockburn, Pearl Jam ("Even Flow"), Maybelle Carter ("When the Springtime Comes Again"), Doc Watson ("Sitting on Top of the World" and "Train That Carried My Girl from Town"), Blind Willie McTell ("Statesboro Blues"), and Third Eye Blind ("Graduate"). Skip James often used a variation, *Open Dm* (Open D with string 3 tuned to F), on his famous "Hard Time Killing Floor Blues" and other great blues songs. Slide guitarist Elmore James and Blind Willie Johnson almost always used Open D, and Mississippi Fred McDowell's "You Got to Move" is in Open D.

DADGAD: It is often associated with Laurence Juber, Pierre Bensusan, Davy Graham, Bert Jansch, Richard Thompson, Jeff Tweedy, and Trey Anastasio. Also, listen to Led Zeppelin ("Kashmir" and "Black Mountain Side"—derived from Bert Jansch's "Blackwaterside" but tuned down a half step) and Pink Floyd ("Poles Apart"). DADGAD is used in Celtic and Irish music (the drone effect suits Irish and Scottish pipe music). It's Open D tuning with the third string tuned up to G, which results in an Open Dsus4 chord.

Open C (C–G–C–E–G–C): It's Open D, two frets lower. Elliott Smith used it on "Ballad of Big Nothing" and "Independence Day."

Open E (E–B–E–G♯–B–E): This tuning is the same as Open D, with all the strings tuned two frets higher. For examples, listen to Duane Allman ("Little Martha" and most of his slide tunes), the Black Crowes ("She Talks to Angels"), and many songs on Bob Dylan's *Blood on the Tracks* album ("Buckets of Rain" and "Simple Twist of Fate").

Open G (D–G–D–G–B–D): Keith Richards plays nearly everything the Stones recorded after "Honky Tonk Women" in this tuning, including "Brown Sugar," "Start Me Up," and many more. It has also been used by Joni Mitchell ("Little Green" and "The Circle Game"), the Black Crowes ("Twice as Hard"), Led Zeppelin ("Travelling Riverside Blues" and "In My Time of Dying"), Eric Clapton ("Walking Blues" and "Running on Faith"), and the Who ("Squeeze Box"). Blues slidemen like Muddy Waters ("Rollin' and Tumblin'" and other early recordings), Ron Wood (when playing with the Stones), George Thorogood, and Son House often used Open G tuning. Robert Johnson capoed up a few frets, or tuned to Open A (the same as Open G, but two frets higher).

Nashville Tuning or High-Strung Guitar (E–A–D–G–B–E): The lowest four strings are taken from a twelve-string guitar set so they are an octave higher than usual. Nashville tuning is used for rhythm guitar in some country, rock, and pop recordings. The chord shapes are the same as standard tuning.

ABOUT THE AUTHOR

FRED SOKOLOW is a versatile "musician's musician." Besides fronting his own jazz, bluegrass, and rock bands, Fred has toured with Bobbie Gentry, Jim Stafford, Tom Paxton, Ian Whitcomb, Jody Stecher, and the Limeliters, playing guitar, banjo, mandolin, and Dobro. His music has been heard on many TV shows (*Survivor*, *Dr. Quinn*), commercials, and movies (listen for his Dixieland-style banjo in *The Cat's Meow*).

Sokolow has written nearly a hundred stringed instrument books and videos for seven major publishers. This library of instructional material, which teaches jazz, rock, bluegrass, country, and blues guitar, banjo, Dobro, and mandolin, is sold on six continents. He also teaches musical seminars on the West Coast. Two jazz CDs, two rock guitar and two banjo recordings, which showcase Sokolow's technique, all received excellent reviews in the U.S. and Europe.

If you think Sokolow still isn't versatile enough, know the he emceed for Carol Doda at San Francisco's legendary Condor Club, accompanied a Russian balalaika virtuoso at the swank Bonaventure Hotel in L.A., won the *Gong Show*, played lap steel and banjo on the *Tonight Show*, picked Dobro with Chubby Checker, and played mandolin with Rick James.

Fred Sokolow and Hal Leonard Publications offer many genre-specific roadmaps books/CDs to enhance your understanding of various musical styles:

- Fretboard Roadmaps for Blues Guitar
- Fretboard Roadmaps for Jazz Guitar
- Fretboard Roadmaps for Rock Guitar
- Fretboard Roadmaps for Country Guitar
- Fretboard Roadmaps for Bluegrass/Folk Guitar
- Fretboard Roadmaps for Slide Guitar
- Fretboard Roadmaps for Acoustic Guitar
- Fretboard Roadmaps for Dobro Guitar
- Fretboard Roadmaps for 5-String Banjo
- Fretboard Roadmaps for Mandolin
- Fretboard Roadmaps for Ukulele
- Fretboard Roadmaps for Bass Guitar
- Fretboard Roadmaps for Guitar (for beginners to music theory)

Direct questions you may have about this book or other Fred Sokolow books to *Sokolowmusic.com*.

Happy navigating!

GUITAR NOTATION LEGEND

Guitar music can be notated three different ways: on a *musical staff*, in *tablature*, and in *rhythm slashes*.

RHYTHM SLASHES are written above the staff. Strum chords in the rhythm indicated. Use the chord diagrams found at the top of the first page of the transcription for the appropriate chord voicings. Round noteheads indicate single notes.

THE MUSICAL STAFF shows pitches and rhythms and is divided by bar lines into measures. Pitches are named after the first seven letters of the alphabet.

TABLATURE graphically represents the guitar fingerboard. Each horizontal line represents a string, and each number represents a fret.

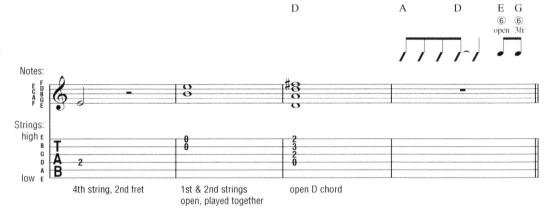

4th string, 2nd fret

1st & 2nd strings open, played together

open D chord

DEFINITIONS FOR SPECIAL GUITAR NOTATION

HALF-STEP BEND: Strike the note and bend up 1/2 step.

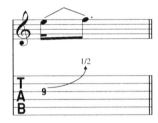

WHOLE-STEP BEND: Strike the note and bend up one step.

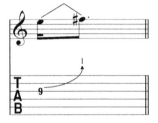

GRACE NOTE BEND: Strike the note and immediately bend up as indicated.

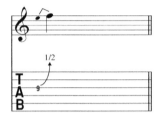

SLIGHT (MICROTONE) BEND: Strike the note and bend up 1/4 step.

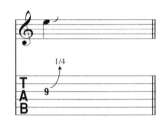

BEND AND RELEASE: Strike the note and bend up as indicated, then release back to the original note. Only the first note is struck.

PRE-BEND: Bend the note as indicated, then strike it.

PRE-BEND AND RELEASE: Bend the note as indicated. Strike it and release the bend back to the original note.

UNISON BEND: Strike the two notes simultaneously and bend the lower note up to the pitch of the higher.

VIBRATO: The string is vibrated by rapidly bending and releasing the note with the fretting hand.

WIDE VIBRATO: The pitch is varied to a greater degree by vibrating with the fretting hand.

HAMMER-ON: Strike the first (lower) note with one finger, then sound the higher note (on the same string) with another finger by fretting it without picking.

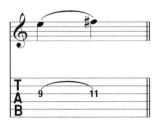

PULL-OFF: Place both fingers on the notes to be sounded. Strike the first note and without picking, pull the finger off to sound the second (lower) note.

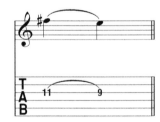

LEGATO SLIDE: Strike the first note and then slide the same fret-hand finger up or down to the second note. The second note is not struck.

SHIFT SLIDE: Same as legato slide, except the second note is struck.

TRILL: Very rapidly alternate between the notes indicated by continuously hammering on and pulling off.

TAPPING: Hammer ("tap") the fret indicated with the pick-hand index or middle finger and pull off to the note fretted by the fret hand.

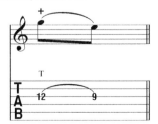

NATURAL HARMONIC: Strike the note while the fret-hand lightly touches the string directly over the fret indicated.

Harm.

12

PINCH HARMONIC: The note is fretted normally and a harmonic is produced by adding the edge of the thumb or the tip of the index finger of the pick hand to the normal pick attack.

P.H.

5

HARP HARMONIC: The note is fretted normally and a harmonic is produced by gently resting the pick hand's index finger directly above the indicated fret (in parentheses) while the pick hand's thumb or pick assists by plucking the appropriate string.

8va - - ¬

H.H.

7(19)

PICK SCRAPE: The edge of the pick is rubbed down (or up) the string, producing a scratchy sound.

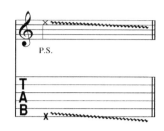

P.S.

MUFFLED STRINGS: A percussive sound is produced by laying the fret hand across the string(s) without depressing, and striking them with the pick hand.

X
X

PALM MUTING: The note is partially muted by the pick hand lightly touching the string(s) just before the bridge.

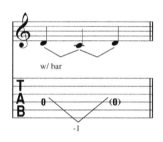

P.M. - - - - - - - - - - - -

0   0   0   0

RAKE: Drag the pick across the strings indicated with a single motion.

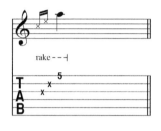

rake - - ¬

5
x
x

TREMOLO PICKING: The note is picked as rapidly and continuously as possible.

5   7

ARPEGGIATE: Play the notes of the chord indicated by quickly rolling them from bottom to top.

5
5
5

VIBRATO BAR DIVE AND RETURN: The pitch of the note or chord is dropped a specified number of steps (in rhythm), then returned to the original pitch.

w/ bar

0   (0)

-1

VIBRATO BAR SCOOP: Depress the bar just before striking the note, then quickly release the bar.

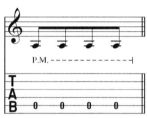

w/ bar - - - - - - - - - ¬

4   5   7

VIBRATO BAR DIP: Strike the note and then immediately drop a specified number of steps, then release back to the original pitch.

-1/2   -1/2   -1/2

w/ bar - - - - - - - - - - - ¬

-1/2   -1/2   -1/2

7   7   7

ADDITIONAL MUSICAL DEFINITIONS

> (accent)	•	Accentuate note (play it louder).
^ (accent)	•	Accentuate note with great intensity.
• (staccato)	•	Play the note short.
⊓	•	Downstroke
V	•	Upstroke
D.S. al Coda	•	Go back to the sign (𝄋), then play until the measure marked "*To Coda*," then skip to the section labelled "**Coda**."
D.C. al Fine	•	Go back to the beginning of the song and play until the measure marked "*Fine*" (end).

Rhy. Fig.	• Label used to recall a recurring accompaniment pattern (usually chordal).
Riff	• Label used to recall composed, melodic lines (usually single notes) which recur.
Fill	• Label used to identify a brief melodic figure which is to be inserted into the arrangement.
Rhy. Fill	• A chordal version of a Fill.
tacet	• Instrument is silent (drops out).
	• Repeat measures between signs.
1. 2.	• When a repeated section has different endings, play the first ending only the first time and the second ending only the second time.

NOTE: Tablature numbers in parentheses mean:
1. The note is being sustained over a system (note in standard notation is tied), or
2. The note is sustained, but a new articulation (such as a hammer-on, pull-off, slide or vibrato) begins, or
3. The note is a barely audible "ghost" note (note in standard notation is also in parentheses).

TRACK SHEET/SONG INDEX

HAL•LEONARD®
GUITAR
PLAY-ALONG

INCLUDES
TAB

AUDIO
ACCESS
INCLUDED

This series will help you play your favorite songs quickly and easily. Just follow the tab and listen to the audio to hear how the guitar should sound, and then play along using the separate backing tracks.

Playback tools are provided for slowing down the tempo without changing pitch and looping challenging parts. The melody and lyrics are included in the book so that you can sing or simply follow along.

105. LATIN
00700939............$16.99

106. WEEZER
00700958............$14.99

107. CREAM
00701069............$16.99

108. THE WHO
00701053............$16.99

109. STEVE MILLER
00701054............$19.99

110. SLIDE GUITAR HITS
00701055............$16.99

111. JOHN MELLENCAMP
00701056............$14.99

112. QUEEN
00701052............$16.99

113. JIM CROCE
00701058............$17.99

114. BON JOVI
00701060............$16.99

115. JOHNNY CASH
00701070............$16.99

116. THE VENTURES
00701124............$17.99

117. BRAD PAISLEY
00701224............$16.99

118. ERIC JOHNSON
00701353............$16.99

119. AC/DC CLASSICS
00701356............$17.99

120. PROGRESSIVE ROCK
00701457............$14.99

121. U2
00701508............$16.99

122. CROSBY, STILLS & NASH
00701610............$16.99

123. LENNON & McCARTNEY ACOUSTIC
00701614............$16.99

124. SMOOTH JAZZ
00200664............$16.99

125. JEFF BECK
00701687............$17.99

126. BOB MARLEY
00701701............$17.99

127. 1970S ROCK
00701739............$16.99

128. 1960S ROCK
00701740............$14.99

129. MEGADETH
00701741............$17.99

130. IRON MAIDEN
00701742............$17.99

131. 1990S ROCK
00701743............$14.99

132. COUNTRY ROCK
00701757............$15.99

133. TAYLOR SWIFT
00701894............$16.99

134. AVENGED SEVENFOLD
00701906............$16.99

135. MINOR BLUES
00151350............$17.99

136. GUITAR THEMES
00701922............$14.99

137. IRISH TUNES
00701966............$15.99

138. BLUEGRASS CLASSICS
00701967............$17.99

139. GARY MOORE
00702370............$16.99

140. MORE STEVIE RAY VAUGHAN
00702396............$17.99

141. ACOUSTIC HITS
00702401............$16.99

142. GEORGE HARRISON
00237697............$17.99

143. SLASH
00702425............$19.99

144. DJANGO REINHARDT
00702531............$16.99

145. DEF LEPPARD
00702532............$19.99

146. ROBERT JOHNSON
00702533............$16.99

147. SIMON & GARFUNKEL
14041591............$16.99

148. BOB DYLAN
14041592............$16.99

149. AC/DC HITS
14041593............$17.99

150. ZAKK WYLDE
02501717............$19.99

151. J.S. BACH
02501730............$16.99

152. JOE BONAMASSA
02501751............$19.99

153. RED HOT CHILI PEPPERS
00702990............$19.99

155. ERIC CLAPTON – FROM THE ALBUM UNPLUGGED
00703085............$16.99

156. SLAYER
00703770............$19.99

157. FLEETWOOD MAC
00101382............$17.99

159. WES MONTGOMERY
00102593............$19.99

160. T-BONE WALKER
00102641............$17.99

161. THE EAGLES – ACOUSTIC
00102659............$17.99

162. THE EAGLES HITS
00102667............$17.99

163. PANTERA
00103036............$17.99

164. VAN HALEN 1986-1995
00110270............$17.99

165. GREEN DAY
00210343............$17.99

166. MODERN BLUES
00700764............$16.99

167. DREAM THEATER
00111938............$24.99

168. KISS
00113421............$17.99

169. TAYLOR SWIFT
00115982............$16.99

170. THREE DAYS GRACE
00117337............$16.99

171. JAMES BROWN
00117420............$16.99

172. THE DOOBIE BROTHERS
00116970............$16.99

173. TRANS-SIBERIAN ORCHESTRA
00119907............$19.99

174. SCORPIONS
00122119............$16.99

175. MICHAEL SCHENKER
00122127............$17.99

176. BLUES BREAKERS WITH JOHN MAYALL & ERIC CLAPTON
00122132............$19.99

177. ALBERT KING
00123271............$16.99

178. JASON MRAZ
00124165............$17.99

179. RAMONES
00127073............$16.99

180. BRUNO MARS
00129706............$16.99

181. JACK JOHNSON
00129854............$16.99

182. SOUNDGARDEN
00138161............$17.99

183. BUDDY GUY
00138240............$17.99

184. KENNY WAYNE SHEPHERD
00138258............$17.99

185. JOE SATRIANI
00139457............$17.99

186. GRATEFUL DEAD
00139459............$17.99

187. JOHN DENVER
00140839............$17.99

188. MÖTLEY CRUE
00141145............$17.99

189. JOHN MAYER
00144350............$17.99

190. DEEP PURPLE
00146152............$17.99

191. PINK FLOYD CLASSICS
00146164............$17.99

192. JUDAS PRIEST
00151352............$17.99

193. STEVE VAI
00156028............$19.99

194. PEARL JAM
00157925............$17.99

195. METALLICA: 1983-1988
00234291............$19.99

196. METALLICA: 1991-2016
00234292............$19.99

HAL•LEONARD®

For complete songlists, visit
Hal Leonard online at
www.halleonard.com

Get Better at Guitar

...with these Great Guitar Instruction Books from Hal Leonard!

101 GUITAR TIPS
INCLUDES TAB
STUFF ALL THE PROS KNOW AND USE
by Adam St. James
This book contains invaluable guidance on everything from scales and music theory to truss rod adjustments, proper recording studio set-ups, and much more.
00695737 Book/Online Audio $16.99

AMAZING PHRASING
INCLUDES TAB
by Tom Kolb
This book/audio pack explores all the main components necessary for crafting well-balanced rhythmic and melodic phrases. It also explains how these phrases are put together to form cohesive solos. The companion audio contains 89 demo tracks, most with full-band backing.
00695583 Book/Online Audio $19.99

ARPEGGIOS FOR THE MODERN GUITARIST
INCLUDES TAB
by Tom Kolb
Using this no-nonsense book with online audio, guitarists will learn to apply and execute all types of arpeggio forms using a variety of techniques, including alternate picking, sweep picking, tapping, string skipping, and legato.
00695862 Book/Online Audio $19.99

BLUES YOU CAN USE
by John Ganapes
This comprehensive source for learning blues guitar is designed to develop both your lead and rhythm playing. Includes: 21 complete solos • blues chords, progressions and riffs • turnarounds • movable scales and soloing techniques • string bending • utilizing the entire fingerboard • and more.
00142420 Book/Online Media................................$19.99

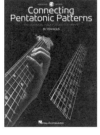

CONNECTING PENTATONIC PATTERNS
INCLUDES TAB
by Tom Kolb
If you've been finding yourself trapped in the pentatonic box, this book is for you! This hands-on book with online audio offers examples for guitar players of all levels, from beginner to advanced. Study this book faithfully, and soon you'll be soloing all over the neck with the greatest of ease.
00696445 Book/Online Audio $19.99

FRETBOARD MASTERY
INCLUDES TAB
by Troy Stetina
Untangle the mysterious regions of the guitar fretboard and unlock your potential. This book familiarizes you with all the shapes you need to know by applying them in real musical examples, thereby reinforcing and reaffirming your newfound knowledge.
00695331 Book/Online Audio $19.99

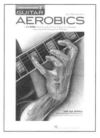

GUITAR AEROBICS
INCLUDES TAB
by Troy Nelson
Here is a daily dose of guitar "vitamins" to keep your chops fine tuned! Musical styles include rock, blues, jazz, metal, country, and funk. Techniques taught include alternate picking, arpeggios, sweep picking, string skipping, legato, string bending, and rhythm guitar.
00695946 Book/Online Audio $19.99

GUITAR CLUES
INCLUDES TAB
OPERATION PENTATONIC
by Greg Koch
Whether you're new to improvising or have been doing it for a while, this book/audio pack will provide loads of delicious licks and tricks that you can use right away, from volume swells and chicken pickin' to intervallic and chordal ideas.
00695827 Book/Online Audio $19.99

PAT METHENY – GUITAR ETUDES
INCLUDES TAB
Over the years, in many master classes and workshops around the world, Pat has demonstrated the kind of daily workout he puts himself through. This book includes a collection of 14 guitar etudes he created to help you limber up, improve picking technique and build finger independence.
00696587..$15.99

PICTURE CHORD ENCYCLOPEDIA
This comprehensive guitar chord resource for all playing styles and levels features five voicings of 44 chord qualities for all twelve keys – 2,640 chords in all! For each, there is a clearly illustrated chord frame, as well as *an actual photo* of the chord being played!.
00695224..$19.99

RHYTHM GUITAR 365
INCLUDES TAB
by Troy Nelson
This book provides 365 exercises – one for every day of the year! – to keep your rhythm chops fine tuned. Topics covered include: chord theory; the fundamentals of rhythm; fingerpicking; strum patterns; diatonic and non-diatonic progressions; triads; major and minor keys; and more.
00103627 Book/Online Audio $24.99

SCALE CHORD RELATIONSHIPS
INCLUDES TAB
by Michael Mueller & Jeff Schroedl
This book/audio pack explains how to: recognize keys • analyze chord progressions • use the modes • play over nondiatonic harmony • use harmonic and melodic minor scales • use symmetrical scales • incorporate exotic scales • and much more!
00695563 Book/Online Audio $14.99

SPEED MECHANICS FOR LEAD GUITAR
INCLUDES TAB
by Troy Stetina
Take your playing to the stratosphere with this advanced lead book which will help you develop speed and precision in today's explosive playing styles. Learn the fastest ways to achieve speed and control, secrets to make your practice time really count, and how to open your ears and make your musical ideas more solid and tangible.
00699323 Book/Online Audio $19.99

TOTAL ROCK GUITAR
INCLUDES TAB
by Troy Stetina
This comprehensive source for learning rock guitar is designed to develop both lead and rhythm playing. It covers: getting a tone that rocks • open chords, power chords and barre chords • riffs, scales and licks • string bending, strumming, and harmonics • and more.
00695246 Book/Online Audio $19.99

Guitar World Presents
STEVE VAI'S GUITAR WORKOUT
INCLUDES TAB
In this book, Steve Vai reveals his path to virtuoso enlightenment with two challenging guitar workouts – one 10-hour and one 30-hour – which include scale and chord exercises, ear training, sight-reading, music theory, and much more.
00119643..$14.99